'Rob has done it again! *The Sixty Minute Grandparent* manages to be both inspirational and practical; humorous and compassionate (at times bringing tears to our eyes); full of wisdom and always rooted in real life stories – all in a book that can be read in the time it takes to have a long, relaxing bath! As grandparents ourselves we want to say, "This is an essential read." Rob's book will give you the confidence to be the sort of grandparent who lets their grandchildren know they have someone who always looks for the best in them, while at the same time giving those same children's parents the support they need. Another wonderful addition to the legendary family of *Sixty Minute* books by Rob.'

Nicky and Sila Lee, authors of *The Parenting Book*

'This is a remarkable book. If you have children, buy it as a gift for your parents now! They will be so glad you did – and you and your children will too!'

Katharine Hill, author of *Rules of Engagement*

'A significant book, pithy and poignant . . . a must read for every grandparent and "would-be" grandparent.'

Positive Parenting

Also by Rob Parsons

The Sixty Minute Father
The Sixty Minute Mother
The Sixty Minute Marriage

The Heart of Success
Loving Against the Odds
Teenagers! What Every Parent Has to Know

The Sixty Minute Grandparent

BECOMING THE BEST GRANDPARENT YOU CAN BE

ROB PARSONS

HODDER & STOUGHTON

To the memory of Ainsley Colstick, a wonderful
husband, father – and grandfather.

First published in Great Britain in 2013 by Hodder & Stoughton
An Hachette UK company

1

Copyright © Rob Parsons, 2013

The right of Rob Parsons to be identified as the Author
of the Work has been asserted by him in accordance with
the Copyright, Designs and Patents Act 1988.

A CIP catalogue record for this title is available from the British Library

ISBN 978 1 444 74569 6
eBook ISBN 978 1 444 74571 9

Typeset in Sabon by Hewer Text UK Ltd, Edinburgh

Printed and bound in the UK by Clays Ltd, St Ives plc

Hodder & Stoughton policy is to use papers that are natural, renewable
and recyclable products and made from wood grown in sustainable
forests. The logging and manufacturing processes are expected to
conform to the environmental regulations of the country of origin.

Hodder & Stoughton Ltd
338 Euston Road
London NW1 3BH

www.hodderfaith.com

'Grandma always made you feel like she had been waiting to see just you all day and now the day was complete.'

Marcy DeMaree

This is a *Sixty Minute* book. If you are quick you can read it in an hour. If you don't have an hour then every so often there are 'Sixty Second Pages' that highlight some key points. Here is wisdom gleaned from hundreds of grandparents, from Brighton to Bangkok, from Sidcup to Sydney. All have been there, done that, got the T-shirt, and all survived to tell the tale – to you.

Contents

Acknowledgements

Most authors will acknowledge that the name on the front cover represents a team of people who have all been part of the creation of their book – and I am glad to be one such. Special thanks to Becky Parsons, Katie Clarke, Michael Bates, Samantha Callan, Kate Hancock, Steve and Gill Williams, Rob and Marion White, the whole team at Care for the Family, my agent Eddie Bell of the Bell Lomax Moreton Agency, and Ian Metcalfe and the team at Hodder & Stoughton. Sheron Rice is indispensable to me and again I am glad to acknowledge her incredible help in another book. Finally, to my wife, Dianne, thanks for all the input, the ideas, the laughs and the endless patience.

1

Dispelling the Myths

They told me that Steve Martin's film *Father of the Bride* was a comedy. I went to see it – and cried. By the time the sequel came along I thought I was safe – after all, like George in the first film, I had, by now, surely got over the sight of my daughter walking off on the arm of another man. Steve Martin couldn't hurt me again. I was wrong. *Father of the Bride Part II* is even more poignant. The scene is set a few years later and George gets the news that his daughter is pregnant. He does his best to look pleased, but in an aside we hear his real feelings: 'First that runt steals my daughter, and now he makes a grandpa out of me!'

George never really comes to terms with the tag 'Granddad', but he does eventually discover the truth of that old bumper sticker: 'If I'd known that having grandchildren was so much fun, I'd have had them first.' I agree. But like most wonderful things in life, being a grandparent is not *all* fun. However, we can at least learn from each other's triumphs – and mistakes. I'd like to share some lessons learnt from old hands at the grandparenting game that I've come across in the twenty-five years I have worked with the national charity Care for the Family. During that quarter of a century I have spoken to almost a million people in live events across the world and worked with all kinds of families – couples, single parents, blended families, parents of children with additional needs and those experiencing the trauma of bereavement. Over the years I have had the privilege of listening to the stories of many different family members and some of the most fascinating are those of the grandparents who, having done it all themselves, now watch from the sidelines as their own children follow them into the role of parenthood.

I have written this book for every grandparent, but I wonder if there is anybody reading this who is about to step into those shoes for the first time and has been told by friends how great it is. Perhaps you are saying to yourself, 'I can't wait. Let me read up about it now before it happens. I'm going to be *Super-Gran/Grand-dad*!'

If that's your situation, it's good that you'll be meeting some old hands in this book first – because although it is true that the 'Funfair of Grandparenting' is wonderful, as with all great rides there are some things we shouldn't forget. First, there are some basic 'safety' rules – ignore these and you'll end up in the 'First Aid for Grandparents' tent thinking, 'What happened?'

And second, it's as well to know the opening hours. There's no point turning up when you're not expected, and perhaps, at that particular moment, not *wanted*, to find the park is closed – at least to you.

Perhaps, at the very beginning of the book, there are a few other things worth mentioning too. The first is that many grandparents I've spoken to have told me that the 'fun' element is somewhat exaggerated. Of course, being a grandparent is brilliant and we wouldn't be without the grandchildren, but the truth is that many of us have never got over the shock of our children having sex, let alone kids. We remember with stunning clarity the moment our dearest told us the news: 'Mum, Dad – Laura and I are having a baby.' Looking back we are sure that we smiled, we are convinced that the words that came out of our mouths were affirming – we seem to recall mumbling, 'A baby!' (as if it were one of several possibilities – a giraffe, for example) and 'Wonderful!' But some of us can remember just as clearly that as our mouths were uttering platitudes, our brains were trying to handle hundreds of other thoughts: 'Yipes! Poor kid!' or, 'Never mind having children – did you finish that geography homework?' and most of all, 'It would have been nice to have been asked. I'm not sure I'm ready for this.'

While we're at it, it may be worth dispelling some of the myths of grandparenting – such as, 'You get none of the responsibilities of parenthood.' Try telling that to the tens of thousands of grandparents who provide free childcare year in, year out. In fact, grandparents provide over 40 per cent of childcare for parents who are at work or studying, and over 70 per cent of childcare the rest of the time,[1] at an annual worth of four billion pounds.[2] Or what about the line, 'Grandparenting is great because you have just the best bits of being with children'? Well, again, not always. The truth is that the little joys are just as likely to throw a wobbly in the aisles of Asda for you as they are for their parents. The only difference is that you have to deal with the discipline not necessarily as you feel is right, but in a way that your children would approve of. As one grandfather said, 'If you think you didn't have control of your own children, wait until you get grandkids!'

Perhaps the greatest myth of all is, 'You can always give them back.' Well, that's not always the case, and certainly sometimes you can't do it fast enough. And occasionally, of course, in cases of family break-up, when you do have to give them back it is in much too final a way.

But once we have dispelled the myths, we can see grandparenting as it was meant to be: a source of joy, in the new life that has come and in seeing that child grow; an opportunity to support our children in the sacred task of parenting; and a chance to pass on stories and values that give roots to young lives. As well as all that, there is also the incredible privilege of being made to feel a little younger by being exposed to the sheer wonder, honesty and unpredictability of children.

All kinds of grandparents

Finally, and perhaps most importantly, there's just one more thing to remember: *there are all kinds of grandparents*. Yes, there are still grandfathers who, after ten minutes with little Amy and Jack, slip back out to the allotment and leave them with Grandma – who interrupts her baking, wipes the flour from her hands onto her pinafore and gathers them to her bosom for a story. But there are also grandmothers who play in rock bands, run multinational corporations, and sky-dive; and there are grandfathers who are still under the impression that they should be asked for ID when they buy a bottle of wine in the local supermarket.

But there are deeper differences than these. There are grandparents who want to be involved as much as possible, and some who are scared to death that they might have to be. There are grandparents who are bursting with energy and relish the thought of a new role, and others who are so tired they can hardly get themselves out of bed, never mind chase a two-year-old around a park. There are grandparents who feel confident about the tasks ahead, and those who are fearful they might make a dreadful mistake: they lie in bed imagining the police searching for the toddler they have managed to lose in Marks and Spencer's. There are grandparents who can't wait to spend as much time as they can with the new arrival, and others who, while wanting to support their children as much as possible, feel they are only just recovering from the trauma of bringing *them* up. They don't feel at all ready to enter the fray again too quickly. Indeed, in one survey, 39 per cent agreed with the statement: 'Now my own children have grown up, I want a life that is free from too many family duties.'[3]

All kinds of grandparents, with all kinds of hopes, fears and expectations: some up for the role, some scared to death of it; some wanting total involvement, some not quite so sure; some feeling it's been too long coming and others shell-shocked that it's arrived. And there are some who, because of the early breakdown of their child's relationship, are afraid they will lose the opportunity to know their grandchildren at all.

But although different, each of us has the same aspiration: to be the best grandparent that we can be. Not the best grandparent according to the standards of other grandparents, friends and so-called 'experts', or even of our children, but of a far more testing judge. It is a standard set by those who will forgive almost anything – from facial hair to picking them up from school in a three-wheeled Reliant Robin – so long as they believe in their hearts the two things that really matter to a child:

'My Gran and Granddad love me.'

'Granny and Grandpa are always there for me.'

2

The Grandparenting Steeplechase

If running the race of grandparenting is like the Grand National – long and with many obstacles – then many of us will fall at one of the first five hurdles. A fall here is not usually terminal and we can get back on the horse, but because it often happens at a time of high emotion, the stakes are high and mistakes are remembered for longer. For over a quarter of a century, I have had the privilege of listening to the advice of grandparents as to how to make it safely to Fence Number 6. Allow me to share some of that received wisdom with you.

Fence Number 1 – Our hopes and dreams

Rachel and her mum, Anne, were having coffee. So far it had been a great day. They had found a birthday present for Rachel's husband, they had ambled through the sales and generally just enjoyed a girls' day out. However, Rachel knew there was something wrong. Ever since childhood she had been able to tell when her mother wanted to talk to her about something but wasn't quite sure how to bring it up. So far today her mother had made three false starts that had ended with, 'Oh . . . nothing.'

But now, in the coffee shop, Rachel's antennae were telling her that her mother was gearing up for another attempt. Her instincts weren't wrong. Her mother coughed twice and then blurted it out: 'So when are you going to make me a grandmother then?'

The look on Rachel's face should have warned her mother to stop right there, but it was as if, now the dam was breached, there was no stopping her. 'The clock is ticking, you know.' Still no response from her daughter – apart from a tear welling up in her left eye.

Stop now, Anne! Stop now! Say, 'Sorry, it's none of my business really.' Get up, pay for your coffee and cream cakes and press on to the next shop . . .

But Anne was committed. She had rehearsed this conversation in her mind dozens of times in the past fortnight; she had talked it over with her husband, and had even arranged the shopping trip so that she might give space for it to occur. She decided to fire the last weapon in her armoury: 'Well, you don't want to be on your own when you're old, do you?'

So now it was done: all the arguments why Rachel and Peter should have children – and soon – were out in the open. So why did things feel so strange? Why did

Anne sense this yawning emotional gap between herself and her daughter? Why this awful silence?

Nothing was said, because there was nothing to *be* said. Rachel didn't need a shopping trip to discover that her mother wanted her to start a family. She and Peter had had endless conversations about when, how and, yes, sometimes if. Did her mother think that she had never heard that clock ticking? Did she think that all the arguments she raised had not already gone through Rachel's mind a hundred times?

But Rachel didn't want to be unkind. Finally she quickly brushed away the tear and said, 'Perhaps one day, Mum. Let's make a move, shall we?'

Fence Number 2 – Getting the news

If you are of a certain age, then you will know where you were when John F. Kennedy was assassinated. If you missed that momentous event, then you may recall with stunning clarity what you were doing when the news broke that Diana, Princess of Wales, had died in a Paris underpass. Who knows what future news stories are of such significance that they will forever be timed and dated in your memory? I guarantee at least one other: the moment your child tells you that there's a baby on the way.

If that event is still in the future, let me warn you now: you will have only one chance to react to this news. For that very reason, practise in front of the bathroom mirror not just what you will say, but how you will *look* when that occasion arrives. Try out various expressions

– smiles, idiotic laughs, wide-eyed incredulity – until you come up with one that conveys *joy*. For just as you will always remember this occasion, it is probable that your child will remember your reaction – especially if it's a negative one – for ever.

If you don't really approve of your child's partner, this would be a great time to put that aside. The birth of a child can be a wonderful opportunity to mend fences. (And comments such as 'Can you afford it?' or 'I thought you were saving for a Ford Focus?' are not recommended.) In fact, just in case you are, at the moment, only a *potential* grandparent and reading this book to get ahead of the game, let me give you two words that will stand you in great stead when that incredible event occurs. Begin practising them now. They are, simply, 'Wow!' and 'Brilliant!' Anything less will look churlish; anything more and you run the risk of verbal diarrhoea and may find yourself raising the subject of the Ford Focus.

Of course, there are situations where the pregnancy is a shock, even a sadness – at least at the time – to all parties, including the new parents. What our children need then is not so much our joy as our unconditional love and support, and to know, above all, that we are with them in this.

Fence Number 3 – During the pregnancy
Make sure you respect your children's feelings. Sometimes they will share the news with you long before they want others to know – and for all kinds of

reasons. Keeping the secret is agony, but we have to do it. Resist even the little hints: 'I can't say much, Angela, but we are soon to hear the patter of tiny feet . . .' And, of course, couples are often, and understandably, nervous about whether all will be well and will want to wait until, say, after the first thirteen weeks of pregnancy and the first scan before 'making the announcement'. It's wise not to start buying gifts too early.

So many people have told us that the hardest thing about the role of grandparenting is to know when to speak and when to stay quiet. The pregnancy is a great time to practise getting that right. Our children may be very keen on a home birth or on an elective caesarean, but whatever our own feelings, our task here must be to support the couple in their decision. Having said this, the bond between a woman and her mother is very strong, and often especially close during a pregnancy, so her mum can get away with – and may even be asked for – a bit of advice given over a cup of coffee that a mother-in-law dare not attempt.

Forgive me moving the scene from horse racing to athletics, but the role of the grandparent during pregnancy – and probably all through the grandchild's life – is to be in the stands shouting encouragement to those who are actually running the parenting race. That word 'encouragement' is absolutely vital. Pregnancy can be a time of such self-doubt. I remember my wife, Dianne, saying when she was six months pregnant with our daughter, Katie, 'I don't think I'm ready to have this child.' With incredible male compassion, I replied, 'It's a bit late for that now!' Take time to tell the prospective mum what a good mother she will be; tell the partner that he will be a great dad. And lastly, during the pregnancy, avoid stories of horrific past births or depressing comparisons: 'Emma was still jogging the day before she gave birth: her waters broke in the Pilates class!'

It can be a good idea to talk to your children before the birth of the baby and say something like, 'Look you're going to be new parents, but we're going to be new grandparents and we'll be learning on the job too. We want to be there for you and help as much as we can; but we don't want to interfere or get in the way. So if we get it wrong a bit, just tell us. You're the parents and what we want most is to support you.' The good thing about this is that it brings the issue of your role (and the risk of your unintentionally overstepping the mark!) into the open.

Fence Number 4 – The birth

You have paced the room, made seventeen cups of tea and pruned the geraniums for the tenth time, but eventually the news comes. Two tips for this crucial phase: first, remember the *joy* bit. Don't be like the mother whose son already had a daughter and was desperately hoping for a boy. When her son told her that Ellie had a little sister, the mother said, 'Oh, lovely . . . Well, we all have to take what we're given.' Even names can be a contentious issue. It's worth remembering that they may not be joking when they tell you the name they have chosen. Better to say, 'Rooney? Perfect!' and risk looking naïve, than to have to dig yourself out of a hole when you belatedly realise they are serious.

Second, don't rush straight to the hospital. Don't visit unless invited. The time after a birth can, and should, be a time of bonding for the new family. And if you're the father's parents it will, perhaps, save you from a little hurt if you realise that it's quite normal that after her husband, the next person a new mum will want to spend time with may well be her own mother.

With so many people involved, it's as well to remember that it's not a competition – for best gifts, most visits, or who the child most looks like. So when you see the child for the first time, try to resist the temptation to bag this new baby for your side of the family with comments like, 'Oh, look at that chin. He's a Wingsbottom!' All that's required is, 'What a beautiful baby!' Nor is this the time to mention unusual features. 'What a conk!' may well be true, but is generally not a good way to start.

Fence Number 5 – The first few weeks

One of the most difficult decisions for any grandparent is how involved to be in the weeks following the birth – especially if geography allows easy visiting. It's not hard to understand why we would want to visit as much as possible. We're excited. And we genuinely want to help. But those two things can easily conspire to cause an almighty fall at the fifth hurdle.

In some situations the father may not be involved during this time, and then it's vital that family and friends gather around Mum to give all the support that's needed. But when the baby's parents are together, there's a very important dynamic that we dare not ignore. Psychologists and paediatricians talk of the importance of what they refer to as 'the cocooning process'. This is a period just after the birth when the couple and their baby need time together to bond as a family.

It's true, especially at the birth of a first child or if the birth has been particularly difficult, that both parents may need as much help as they can get. But even then, that help has to be given in a way that supports, not suffocates. The couple still need time alone. And don't be surprised if a woman turns to her mother first when she wants extra support. This is both normal and understandable, and is probably a time for the husband's parents to stand back a little.

Of course we want to visit as much as possible. We want to help – and 'just have a quick cuddle, while I'm here'. But sometimes the help that is born out of such good intentions can become claustrophobic for the new parents. In medieval times criminals were put in stocks and pillories, their heads, arms or legs secured tightly. Apparently one poor soul complained that the biggest problem was not that people threw rotten eggs at him, but that his relatives could visit when he had no chance of getting away. It can feel a bit like that for new parents after the birth of a baby. They are at the mercy of anybody who knocks on their door bearing a cuddly toy and a knitted hat.

It can get very crowded indeed. As well as friends and other relatives, there may be other grandparents – maternal and paternal, step-grandparents, even great-grandparents – all wanting to see the brand-new arrival. If we're lucky enough to live close to the new parents, we must allow others from further afield space when they visit. There will be plenty of time for us to have cuddles later. The phrase to remember here is the one used at the beginning of *The Purpose Driven Life*,[1] one of the best-selling books of this century: 'It's not about you.'

Although it's certainly true that it's not all about us, the role of a grandparent is, nevertheless, a vital one. The power we have to influence a child's life is very real. In the next few chapters we look at some of the ways we can do that. We begin with the most basic way of all: to help make the roots of this young life *strong*.

Sixty Second Page

🕐 The birth of a child is a great time to mend fences – especially with your child's partner.

🕐 Give a family with a new baby *space*.

🕐 Don't criticise the new parents, even if only by implication: 'Oh, he's never any trouble when *I* have him.'

🕐 Remember that even acts of kindness can be suffocating if there are too many of them.

🕐 Try to build a good relationship with the other set of grandparents and avoid any competition as to who is best or most loved.

🕐 At birthdays and Christmas, try to coordinate present-giving through your grandchildren's parents.

🕐 Remember that times have changed – our children may do it differently, but it can still work. (After all, your children don't rot their baby's teeth with Rosehip Syrup!)

When my granddaughter was five, I took her to pick up a relative who was coming to her birthday party. Aunty Margaret wasn't known for her cheery disposition – in fact, she was generally cross-tempered, disapproving and went about life with her lips pursed. My granddaughter talked excitedly about what my husband and I had given her for her birthday. Aunty Margaret soon interrupted her: 'You're spoilt!' she hissed.

'Yes, I know,' my granddaughter replied after a short pause. 'Grandma and Grandpa do spoil me – *and I like it!'*

3

Who Do You Think You Are?

After the end of the Second World War over two hundred French soldiers were brought home from prison camps with total amnesia because of the torture and deprivations they had suffered. The Red Cross managed to trace the families of most of them, but after several months there were still dozens who had not been 'claimed'. Then somebody had an idea: advertisements were put in national newspapers asking anybody who had a missing relative to come to the Paris Opera House on a certain day. When the time arrived the auditorium was packed with those hoping to find a loved one. Suddenly the house lights went down and the first of the 'lost ones' shuffled onto the stage. He blinked as the spotlights hit his eyes, turned around twice to allow the audience to have a good look at him, and then shouted into the vast expanse of the auditorium the words he had been told to say: 'Does anybody know who I am?'

I remember when I was in my late thirties taking my son, Lloyd, to school one day and him saying, 'Dad, tell me what life was like in the olden days.' He made me feel as if I was part of the story of Robin Hood that I'd been reading to him the night before. But the truth is that 'the olden days' hold a fascination for every child – and for reasons that may not be immediately apparent to them. On the surface they are asking for information about a time they have never experienced, but unknowingly they are searching for answers to one of the most significant questions of life, the one asked in the Paris Opera House all those years ago: 'Who am I?'

Children who say to their mother, 'Where did I come from?' are searching for more than biological answers. As we grow, we want to know what our place is in the world: 'How did I get here – how do I *fit*?' And although in life we are so often consumed with the demands of the present or worries for the future, for answers to some of the very deepest questions we have to go *back*. We have to discover *our roots*.

Nobody can help us more in that task than our grandparents. They are holders of the memories, the stories, the ups and downs of life that have been woven together over generations to make up our family. Those memories can provide part of the structure on which young children can build their life. They help to give a sense of 'belonging' and, therefore, security.

The problem is that before a grandchild is born, grandparents have often come to believe that others don't want to hear those family stories: 'Oh, Dad! Not that old one!' 'Mum! You've told us about that twice this week already!' What our children don't realise is that they can afford to be cavalier about the past only because it has already been deposited safe in the vaults of their minds. But the birth of a grandchild changes everything. These little ones – for seven or eight years at least – will have an almost inexhaustible desire to learn about 'the olden days'. And so they should. Lois Wyse said, 'Grandchildren are the dots that connect the lines from generation to generation.' And fortunately for most children, they will find in a grandparent somebody who is all too willing to take them on that most exhilarating of rides – the journey back in time.

As grandparents we need to have confidence that the past matters. Professor of psychiatry Jack C. Westman puts it like this: 'As grandparents we have important symbolic and practical functions in our cultures. We are important simply for what we mean as the oldest living representatives of our families . . . We are the links to the past in our families. We can recall when the parents of our grandchildren were young, not always to their liking!'[1]

As I have spoken to grandparents all over the world, they have told me time and time again of the sheer joy of sharing the past with their grandchildren. One grandmother took her granddaughter Daisy on a three-hour train journey just so they could see the house in which she grew up as a child in Manchester. When they got to the cul-de-sac the little girl looked on wide-eyed as her grandmother told her about a time when only one person in the whole street owned a car. The grandmother described the games they used to play on the wide expanse of the empty road – 'Poison Ball', 'Bad Eggs' and 'What's The Time Mr Wolf?'

As they walked along the street towards the old house the child was visibly getting more and more excited. 'You look happy,' said her grandmother.

'I am,' said Daisy. 'I'm going to see the bedroom you had when you were a little girl.'

'Oh, I don't think we'll be able to do that, darling. We'll probably just look at the outside of the house,' replied her grandmother. By now they were outside the small front wall of the terraced house. The grandmother hesitated and then thought, 'Oh well, in for a penny, in for a pound,' and rang the bell. A young woman holding a baby answered the door and the second the grandmother saw her smile, she knew that all would be well.

Within moments she and her granddaughter were climbing the stairs together and she heard herself say, 'My room was that one – at the end of the landing. You go and have a look.'

The child opened the bedroom door and gazed in. She was silent for a while and then looked back.

'Do you like it?' her grandmother asked.

'Yes, Nan, but it's very, very small.'

The grandmother laughed out loud. 'Yes, my dear, and there were three of us in there!'

Before the child could respond the young woman downstairs was shouting up, 'Anyone for tea or lemonade?'

Of course it's not just your old home that's of interest to your grandchildren, but anywhere *at all* that was significant to you: your first school, your first job, the first time you kissed their grandfather. Tell them how you *felt* going into that playground or on that first day at work; tell them how your stomach churned with that kiss. Don't let the cynicism of the world rob you or your grandchildren of these moments. Have the courage to grasp hold of them for yourself – and to pass them on.

The 'journey into the past' can be varied and fun. With older children it may mean sifting through the 'treasure chest' in your loft and talking about all the paraphernalia – pictures, letters, bills and clothes – that has been hidden there for years. With this in mind, don't be too clinical in your application of de-cluttering when it comes to the past. Grandchildren need to sift through things that one day their parents will almost certainly discard; don't rob them of that pleasure.

Perhaps the greatest repository of the past is the photo album. Explain to your grandchildren who the people are in those snaps and tell their stories. Show them pictures of their parents – toothless and grinning on assorted beaches – and of fearsome aunties and crazy uncles. One grandmother told us that her granddaughter never tires of looking at her wedding album. Every time the child opens it she says the same thing, 'You were beautiful, Nanny, but Grampy looks funny.'

She said that they always talk about the same things – the car being late, the best man forgetting the ring, how she fluffed her lines.

Places, pictures, stories – and junk. But just one more thing before we leave the past. Grandparents have a duty to preserve it. Professor Westman says, 'We are the repositories of information about our genealogies.'[2] In African culture there is a saying: 'When an old person dies, it is as if a library burns down.' But the library shouldn't burn down. One of the most valuable things a grandparent can do is to record the past for future generations – so make sure *you* record it. I have spoken to grandparents who, on beginning this task, were certain they had little to say. A few months later, however, they had written journals bursting with stories or had recorded hours of memories. And remember, when you do this, it's not your problem to edit out the boring bits; that task is for others, later. Your job is simple: to take out a little fire insurance on that library.

Traditions that get passed on from generation to generation can be part of 'the giving of roots'. Roy Castle was one of Britain's most famous entertainers, perhaps best known for the television show *Record Breakers*. He and his wife, Fiona, had four children. Just before Roy died, Dianne and I spent a night at his home. Before we went to bed we were chatting and he said, 'You know, at the start there is just one pair of shoes by your bed, and then if you get married there are two pairs of shoes. If children come along there are little pairs of shoes alongside yours, and gradually those shoes get bigger and one day they're not there any more. And then there are only two pairs of shoes again and finally . . . just one pair.'

We carried on talking and Roy told us that when he was a child his father used to clean his shoes, and when Roy's own children came along he decided to carry on that little tradition. During the night I wrote a poem about it and read it to Roy and Fiona over breakfast. It seemed to touch him. A few weeks later I went to the London Palladium in the West End to see Roy perform for the last time. Half way through his set he sat on a stool and read the poem . . .

A Man Looks Back

I always cleaned the children's shoes –
the little (tiny!) patent shoes,
that covered feet fresh out of booties –
cleaned the black and made it shine,
removing final traces of stewed prune
and other culinary delights known only to the very
young.

And as they grew, I cleaned a larger shoe.
Shoes that were strong enough to walk in almost!
Certainly strong enough for a toddler to take five
steps . . . and fall.

And then those first school shoes:
shoes that led such little feet
into a world full of such tomorrows.

And later, shoes, the toes of which
lost all their battles with footballs, gravel, and old
tin cans;
new shoes that looked old within a week.

I cleaned them all.

And as each night I did the task,
a million memories came flooding back,
and I remembered a man long gone would clean our
shoes.

Six children in all.
My father cleaned each one,
as I now shine these for mine.

But children grow.
And shoes are for feet that move,
that take the boy into a man.
And I remember well the evening that I came
with cloth and brush as I had done so many times,
only to discover that, of course, the shoes had gone.

But they will come again, those shoes,
come again to me.
Oh, not for cleaning now –
other hands have long since done that task.
No, they will bring a man to me and a woman
holding the hands of tiny ones
with little feet.

And young eyes will look up and say,
'Grandpa, Mummy said . . . that you will clean my
*   shoes.'*

Sixty Second Page

🕐 Grandparents are the 'Keepers of the Past'. Make sure you record your memories.

🕐 When they are old enough, help your grandchildren make a family tree.

🕐 Take time to show your grandchildren your family photo album and explain who's who.

🕐 If possible, take your grandchildren to see your childhood home, or places where you worked or that were special to you.

🕐 Don't throw things out too quickly – letters, clothes, photographs, records, CDs – leave some 'junk' for others to plough through.

🕐 Develop traditions with your grandchildren: 'When we go to Granny and Granddad's house we always . . .'

A grandfather was telling his little grandson about the things he did in his own childhood: swinging from a tyre that hung from a tree, pony riding, skating on the pond, picking blackberries. The boy was wide-eyed, taking this all in, and then gave a sigh: 'I wish I'd got to know you sooner!'

4

The Power of a Grandparent

Lord Soper, the famous socialist, pacifist and Methodist minister, used to preach at Speakers' Corner in Hyde Park. One day somebody yelled out, 'OK, Soper, tell us where the soul is in the body!' Soper hardly missed a beat. 'Oh,' he said, 'it's where the music is in the organ!'

I think being a grandparent is somewhat like that. In some ways we would be forgiven for yelling out, 'Where's the magic in grandparenting?' After all, the component parts may seem rather unimpressive. Perhaps we feel we didn't make a great job of parenting the first time around. Perhaps we get tired pretty easily, or are so 'uncool' we think Coldplay has something to do with making snowmen. Yet at the heart of grandparenting there is a power so strong it can affect the life of a child for ever.

The special bond

Some child development specialists suggest that the key to the positive relationship that many grandparents have with their grandchildren is that a grandparent can appreciate a child's good qualities *without feeling responsible for the bad ones*.[1] That is not to say that grandparents don't care. We may care passionately. It simply means that the task of dealing with the day-to-day difficult issues in our grandchildren's lives lies in the hands of others – those self-same 'others' who so often drove us crazy when *they* were children! That's why one humorist said, 'The reason grandparents and grandchildren get along so well is that they've got a common enemy.'[2]

Psychologists describe the relationship between a grandparent and grandchild as 'an emotionally uncomplicated form of love'.[3] Parents might complain that it's easier for grandparents. They don't have the twenty-four-hour-a-day hassles, the cross patches and, sometimes in the teenage years, the unremitting rudeness that so often comes attached to puberty. Because they don't have to deal with the normal responsibilities of parenthood their task is, in many ways, much easier and the relationship quite different. One child put it like this: 'Being with my nan is like having a bath that is full of bubbles filled with love and with no cold bits.'

The gifts of love and attention are not just emotional trinkets, though. They help the grandchild achieve something absolutely vital for strong growth into adulthood: emotional health. In a world where friends can be cruel and teachers sometimes have to say negative things, it's good to have somebody who believes in you *anyway*.

We dare not underestimate the value of such a friend amidst the challenges of our modern world. The pressures on the young in today's society are unprecedented – and none more so than the pressure to achieve. Children who live in the UK are tested academically more than any others in Europe; the skills that have to be grasped are demanded at an ever-younger age.[4]

Perhaps the most insidious pressure is that of physical attractiveness. In this area in particular the combination of the Internet, exploding media availability and mobile phone technology combine to bombard young minds with messages that are relentless and dangerous. The four-year-old who today makes her grandfather a dinner with plastic saucepans on a plastic cooker and watches as he pretends to devour it with relish will, within five short years, be targeted by companies that want to sell her sexy underwear a padded bra, perhaps. Soon, maybe, they'll be able to target her via her mobile phone. Not old enough to have breasts, but old enough to begin to bear the relentless pressure of being a woman in a world where men will judge her by how she looks. The results of that pressure are evident: a survey of twelve- to eighteen-year-old girls found that more than half hate the way they look, four in ten consider themselves overweight (whatever their actual weight) and more than two-thirds would consider cosmetic surgery.[5] And don't think this just affects girls. Commenting on the explosion in

eating disorders even among boys, one expert said,
'These days it's not enough to be an ace footballer – you
have to be a great-looking ace footballer.'[6]

Building confidence

One of the reasons why grandparents can be such a
force for good is that in their early years children are
open to messages that often affect how they feel about
themselves for a lifetime. Grandparents have the incredible privilege of helping to sow seeds that lead to healthy
self-esteem and self-assurance in children – qualities
that they can later use to stand against peer pressure
and commercial exploitation.

So what are the good messages we can pass on? There
are hundreds to choose from. And grandparents, above
all, use them so generously and so liberally – especially
when their grandchildren are young: 'You look lovely
today', 'I think you could end up playing for Manchester United', 'You're a wonderful cook' (to that
four-year-old and her plastic three-course dinner).

Are these statements all true? No. Are they lies? No.
Because grandparents live in a world where the best is
always searched for – and where the comparisons that
others make don't matter a jot. Do the children believe
the judgement? When they are young – yes. When they
are older – maybe not. But that later realism will rob
the words of none of their power, for by then they will
have done their job.

As grandchildren get older, grandparents can help
them face failure head on, pick themselves up and make

sure they understand that failing in a certain task doesn't make them a failure as a person. But whatever age their grandchild is, the grandparents' task is to make a young person feel special and significant – and, in so doing, form a bulwark against the onslaught of voices that will try with all their might to demand results in order to give acceptance.

Someone who is there for you

The giving of these two attributes – love and attention – need not be complicated. In fact it's almost scandalous how *little* a grandparent can get away with and still be thought 'the best grandparent in the world'. One eight-year-old said, 'Grandmothers don't have to do anything except *be there*.'

Of course, many grandparents might reply, 'Nice! I collect them at 8.30 a.m., take them to gym, to the park, to soft play, feed them, change them and drop them back at 5 p.m! No, I don't have to do anything at all.' And those grandparents might be right – except for one thing: that eight-year-old has captured the *heart* of being a grandparent. Many grandparents have to do more – much more – but the essence of grandparenting is to do what uncles, aunties, friends and even parents often don't have the time to do – simply *be there*.

Now, don't panic if you live a long distance away from your grandchild. What I am about to share should be an enormous comfort to all grandparents, because *being there* is not necessarily a geographical thing. Rather, for children (and actually yearned for by every

inevitably comes between grandchildren, and to forge strong bonds. I'm not talking about childcare now – we'll come on to that later. No, here we're talking about reading stories to a three-year-old, or about zoo visits with an eight-year-old, or, wonder of wonders, about a teenager of fourteen, who refuses to speak to anybody else without grunting, being prepared to pour out her heart to a grandfather who has time – time to listen.

Having mentioned teenagers, let me say that I believe the role of a grandparent in an adolescent's life can be remarkable. Superficially the relationship ought not to work, but it frequently does. It seems as if the age gap which so often makes it hard to communicate across the generations helps in this case because it removes any sense of competition or comparison. A grandparent is not a parent, a friend or a teacher and can bring another perspective completely. It can be quite an eye-opener for a fifteen-year-old girl to discover that her grandmother's heart was also broken when *she* was a teenager – and that somehow she got through it. Grandparents don't have to come up with solutions: so often their power is in simply *listening*. Don't underestimate the power of a grandparent in the life of a teenager. Some experts have called grandparents 'an emotional safety net' for teen-agers – somebody who will not just help them get through the teenage years, but who will shape their lives for ever.[8]

But whatever age our grandchildren are, this is not about being able to entertain them so well they would readily choose a chat with us over playing on their

Playstation. That could be a losing wicket. Rather, it's about giving them the dignity of believing that they matter.

I have seen grandparents insist that their grandchildren visit them. They may get what they want, but it's far better if the grandchildren really *want* to see you. Who knows what goes on in the mind of a child that makes them really yearn to visit their grandparents? I once asked my son (that would be my testing, non-compliant, letters-from-the-school son) why he liked visiting my mother so much. He answered in a heartbeat, 'Nanny Mabel does me fried eggs.' I remember thinking, 'Fried eggs? I'm slogging to earn the money to buy you computers, bicycles and holidays, and Nanny Mabel gets an accolade for fried eggs!' My son is now married with children of his own, which may have given him the security to share with me the other day that on one occasion my mother cooked him three of them. Oh dear. Think of the fat, think of the cholesterol, think of his health – and think of the sheer unadulterated fun of knowing somebody so daring she would fry three of the things for one child!

Try to laugh with your grandchildren. Relax a little. You don't bear the ultimate responsibility for them so you don't have to put on the 'cross' face that you sometimes had to pretend to wear with your own children. Keep a box of games handy and (yes, I know it's almost impossible for grandfathers, no matter how young the child) let them win once in a while.

Especially when they are young, we have to be prepared to do the simplest things – often repeating them *time after time*. If they are small, tell them stories and let them join in: 'Once upon a time there was a little boy called Connor. As he was going along the road he saw a . . .'

'Giant banana!' shrieks Connor.

Nan continues, 'Yes, a giant banana. And suddenly the banana turned into a . . .'

It's true you'll have to have your wits about you, so don't do it just after lunch, but the grandkids will love it and will probably repeat the whole thing one day with their own children sat on their laps.

Go to pop concerts with your teenage grandchildren. The fascinating thing is that some teenagers who wouldn't be seen dead out with their parents are quite prepared to drag Gran to hear a pop group like JLS. And it's definitely a good thing to shock your grandchildren occasionally by doing something completely outrageous. I know of one grandfather who dyed his hair pink for the weekend (don't do this if your grandchildren are teenagers: if they copy you, your kids will kill you!). One seven-year-old put it like this: 'My nan is old on the outside, but she acts like she's young on the inside.'

Ah, the power of a grandparent! There are all kinds of grandparents: high-flying ones and ordinary ones, ample ones and skinny ones, studious ones and batty ones. The truth is that so often kids don't care which, for the power of a grandparent lies elsewhere. It may be that their lives are extremely busy, but they make their grandchildren feel as if they are the most important people on the face of the earth. One woman said, 'Grandma always made you feel like she had been waiting to see just you all day and now the day was complete.'⁹ And an eight-year-old, commenting on what was great about her grandmother, put it like this: 'If grandmothers take us for walks they slow down for things like pretty leaves and caterpillars. They never say, "Hurry up" . . . Grandparents are the only grown-ups that have . . . *time*.'

Imagine having someone in your life who never said, 'Hurry up' – someone who had time to dawdle, to draw, to dangle legs in a cold river and tell stories. There's only one thing that could possibly be better than that: someone crazy enough to cook you three fried eggs.

Yes, it's true we can be a force for good in the lives of our grandchildren. But don't get carried away – the pitfalls are frequent, and deep, and none more dangerous than the one we will consider next.

Sixty Second Page

🕐 Grandparents can instil in children a real sense of self-worth and help to build their confidence. This is a crucial defence against a world that demands results in return for acceptance.

🕐 Unconditional love is the most powerful force in the world. In a world that can bully us, measure us, assess us, judge us and demand one more trick when our bag of magic is already empty, a grandparent can be someone who loves us . . . anyway.

🕐 Grandkids don't care how cool you are: they are just pleased that you have time for them – even doing really simple things.

🕐 Spending time with grandchildren *individually* removes the competition and allows an opportunity to get close – to forge strong bonds.

🕐 A grandparent can be an 'emotional safety net' in the life of a teenager. Show your teenage grandchildren that you understand how they are feeling, and keep their confidences.

When You Thought I Wasn't Looking

When you thought I wasn't looking,
I saw you hang my first painting on the refrigerator,
and I immediately wanted to paint another one.

When you thought I wasn't looking,
I saw you feed a stray cat,
and I learned that
it was good to be kind to animals.

When you thought I wasn't looking,
I saw you make my favourite cake for me,
and I learned that the little things can be the special
*   things in life.*

When you thought I wasn't looking,
I heard you say a prayer,
and I knew that there is a God I could always talk
*   to,*
and I learned to trust in Him.

When you thought I wasn't looking,
I saw you make a meal and take it to a friend who
*   was sick,*
and I learned that we all have to help take care of
*   each other.*

When you thought I wasn't looking,
I saw you take care of our house and everyone in it,

and I learned we have to take care of what we are
   given.

When you thought I wasn't looking,
I saw how you handled your responsibilities, even
   when you didn't feel good,
and I learned that I would have to be responsible
   when I grow up.

When you thought I wasn't looking,
I saw tears come from your eyes,
and I learned that sometimes things hurt,
   but it's all right to cry.

When you thought I wasn't looking,
I saw that you cared,
and I wanted to be everything that I could be.

When you thought I wasn't looking,
I learned most of life's lessons that I need to know
to be a good and productive person when I grow up.

When you thought I wasn't looking,
I looked at you and wanted to say,
'Thanks for all the things I saw when you thought I
   wasn't looking.'

5

A Little Interference

In some of the parenting seminars we run at Care for the Family we will often have hundreds of delegates. They will be a mixture of prospective parents and actual parents, as well as grandparents and professionals who work with children and young people. At some time during the day I will talk about the fact that parenting is a 'long-haul' business. To prove that, I tell the story of a ninety-five-year-old woman who came into my office many years ago. She smiled at me and said, 'There, that's done! I can rest in peace now.' I asked her what she had done. She replied, 'I've just managed to get my youngest son into an old people's home.' She wasn't in one herself, but her son was in his mid-seventies and a little shaky. This dear woman of almost a hundred years old was tying up the last few ends – as a mother.

Ironically, it's that unswerving lifelong commitment to care for our children that can lead to one of the greatest mistakes we can make when and if they have children of their own. When they were little we cared passionately about their welfare, but as they got older we had to temper that care and protection with the willingness to allow them the freedom of independence – and therefore even to make mistakes. However, we need to retain that balance not just when our children are truculent teenagers, but when they are parents themselves. Of all the regrets grandparents have shared with me, the ones that are most often mentioned relate to getting the right balance between caring for their children and honouring their children's independence.

It's not hard to understand why a mother who nursed her little girl through chickenpox, mumps and measles, kissed and bandaged knees and extracted tiny splinters from small fingers would have some doubts about trusting her now grown-up daughter and brand-new grandchild to the rugby-playing, 'Can't-find-my-car-keys', 'What's-a-placenta?' husband. But she must. Yes, it will be with prayers and in fear and trembling – but she must.

Of course, there are exceptions: if grandparents believe that their grandchild is in danger – perhaps because of abuse or neglect – then it is their duty to get involved. But those instances aside, we must somehow allow our children to learn to parent in *their* way. One grandmother said, 'Remember that your role on the family team has changed. You aren't the coach any more: you are the president of your children's fan club – your job now is to cheer them on.'

To attempt to fill any other role will almost certainly damage the relationship between you and your children. I think of Carol, a grandmother who was having a conversation with her son and daughter-in-law when suddenly the newborn baby began to cry in the nearby pram. Her son immediately got up, lifted the baby into his arms and began to rock him.

Carol couldn't contain herself: 'You can't keep picking him up, you know. He'll have you running around after him like nobody's business. It won't hurt him to cry for a bit.'

Her daughter-in-law was going to stay quiet, but thought better of it: 'Carol, we have to do what *we* think is right with Liam. He's *our* child.'

Carol bit her lip, but she said to her husband later, 'I'm not welcome around there.'

And the truth was, she was right: she *wasn't* welcome – not as a giver of unasked-for advice, at least. She was welcome to give support, to encourage and to enjoy the sheer thrill of this brand-new baby, but Carol had crossed a line. The fact that she crossed it because of genuine concern for the young couple was of secondary importance. She had moved from care to *control*.

This desire for control is often born out of genuine care, of course. That was the case for the parents of sixteen-year-old Emma, a single parent who gave birth while studying for her GCSEs. After Emma had told them she was pregnant, they had said, 'We'll look after the

baby. You just go back to school and get on with your life.'
But although in the early stages of her pregnancy Emma
had thought that was exactly what she would do, the
second she held Charlie she knew that more than anything
else she wanted to bring him up and be as involved as
possible in every part of his life. Emma had terrific rows
with her parents about her decision to drop out of school
to look after him, but now, ten years later, everybody –
including her mum and dad, who eventually came round
(and were brilliant) – is glad of her determination.

Of course we can sometimes give our children a little
advice with regard to the grandkids, but a good tip I got
from a grandparent of eight children was that the medicine slips down more easily when mixed with the
sweetener of vulnerability. It's a little easier to handle a
baby that's crying half the night if you know that others
have gone through this and come out the other end.
What's not so helpful is a grandfather who says, 'Mmm,
strange. At this age, you were sleeping for twelve straight
hours.' I remember when our daughter, Katie, was
worried that her son, Harry, wasn't eating enough. I
think Dianne was about to churn out the old 'He'll eat
when he's hungry' line, but instead she said, 'Oh, Katie,
I know how you feel. When you were two I took you to
the doctor with exactly the same worry. I was beside
myself – imagining you fading away. The doctor was
about seventy years old; he peered at me over half-moon
glasses and said, "Mrs Parsons, there is no recorded
case of a toddler with food in front of him dying of
hunger."' Dianne and Katie laughed like drains.

Conflict between grandparents and their children over unsought advice can involve many issues, but if the grandparents who speak to us are anything to go by then discipline is the number one. And perhaps in this area more than any other we have to let our children decide what is right. After all, they know exactly what we think in this area – they were on the sharp end of it for eighteen years.

But it's more than that. Wherever possible, we have to present a united front – to back up our children's stance on discipline. If Susie, aged four, asks us for a biscuit while she is staying with us and we know that this is not normally allowed just before tea-time, it's possibly best to say, 'No, we don't have snacks now because it's nearly tea-time.'

When we act like that, we give the child the message that these rules actually do matter. There is something worse than discipline for a child and that is the belief that there are no boundaries – and, even if there are, that nobody cares if they are enforced. This affects a child's fundamental sense of security. It's fair enough to have some of your own rules when they are at your house ('Grandma's house, Grandma's rules'), but overall what our kids say is what has to go. Of course, as grandparents we want to 'spoil' our grandchildren occasionally, but we have to do that without undermining our own children.

Of course, grandparents are full of knowledge that has been built up over many years – veritable encyclopaedias on feeding, sleeping, mumps, chickenpox, vomiting, naughty steps, tantrums and teething. But so many grandparents feel that whenever they give advice, it's rebuffed. The truth is that our children are often bombarded by advice – from healthcare professionals, friends, self-help books, the Internet and occasionally total strangers in the aisles of the supermarket. If we are wise as grandparents we will hold our advice – brilliant though we're sure it is – until that defining moment when it will be welcomed. In other words, *when we're asked for it*. Having said that, really wily grandparents will sometimes manage to slip in a little advice without their kids even realising. One grandmother has a brilliant line: 'Not much good asking me, love, it's all so long ago, it's a bit of a blur . . . but I seem to remember this working . . .'

Ah, that battle between genuine care and control. A grandparent that I met some years ago mucked it up big time. Her children and grandchildren lived in a semi-detached house. One day she waltzed into their living room and exclaimed, 'Good news! I've just agreed to buy the other half of the semi!'

But then I think of another grandmother who won her battle. She had offered to go to live with her daughter and son-in-law for a month after the birth of their first child, but they had declined. At first she was hurt, but then she rallied and cooked a dozen main meals and desserts for their freezer. Now that *was* welcome.

That leads us nicely to the other battleground on which so many grandparents have lost in the war of relationships: the unannounced visit. 'I've just popped in with some vitamins/flowers/cream cakes/Valium.' The truth is that most children are happy to see their parents, and even if in-law relationships aren't completely sweetness and light, they are prepared to welcome grandparents for the sake of the kids. But whether they are just not feeling up to giving hospitality, or are desperate to get little Johnny to bed, there are times when they would rather you didn't just turn up. So it's usually best to telephone first – and the golden rule is that fewer visits that are enjoyed by all are much better than too many that end up being awkward (not to mention that it's embarrassing having to hide behind the sofa until Granddad has got tired of ringing the doorbell).

As we come to the end of this chapter, let me mention a conversation I had while writing this book. Some friends were visiting. I told them about some of the topics I was hoping to cover in *The Sixty Minute Grandparent*. When I got to the issue of grandparents who interfere too much, they went very quiet. To be honest, I thought I might have offended them. I asked, 'Is everything OK? Did I say something wrong?'

The wife looked very sad. She said, 'Oh no, Rob – the book sounds great. It's just that one topic. You see, my girls' grandparents have no interest in them at all. They don't write, they don't ring – it's as if they just don't care. I know my children are missing something that for other children is so very special. If a little over-interference was the price I'd have to pay for them to be more involved in my kids' lives, I think I would willingly pay it.'

I found the conversation very moving. It made me realise that although over-interference is wrong, there is something worse: a grandparent who doesn't seem to care at all.

Sixty Second Page

🕐 Remember there's a borderline between 'care' and 'control' – and grandparents don't have a permit to cross it.

🕐 Our kids can probably survive without our advice, but they desperately need our affirmation. Find things you can praise in your child's parenting.

🕐 Let your children know that it's not just them struggling with some element of parenting: 'Oh, you were much worse than Tom at this age. I used to be up half the night!'

🕐 Don't 'pop in' unannounced unless you are absolutely sure that both parents will welcome this. Give them a quick ring first.

🕐 With a new baby, make sure you don't take over. You may do a better job than your children for a few weeks, but they've got this child for eighteen years. The sooner they start the better.

🕐 Remember that different things work for different people. Some people pick up a baby as soon as it cries, some tough it out. Some feed on demand, some according to the timetable. Parents need to find their own way – and kids are great survivors.

The little boy looked up at his mother: 'When is Nanny coming to visit again? I hope it's soon!'

The mother was so pleased. She hadn't thought the little boy had much affection for his grandmother, who was rather hard to please, even for a five-year-old.

'It's lovely that you want to see Nanny, Simon,' said his mother. 'Why are you so keen for her to visit?'

Her son smiled. 'Because I want to see Daddy do his trick.'

'What trick is that, dear?' asked the mother.

'His Spiderman one,' said Simon.

'His Spiderman trick?' said the mother.

'Yes,' said the small boy. 'I heard Daddy say to Uncle Matt that the next time your mother visits he's going to climb the walls.'

6

The Childcare Dilemma

We are going to think now about the issue of grand-parents who are involved in the care of their grandchildren. In the vast majority of cases this will be a positive choice, taken mainly for financial and personal reasons – their children need to be at work, or commercial childcare is too expensive, or they just don't think it appropriate. But there are many grandparents who do not fall into this category. Looking after their grandchildren for them is not a choice, but a necessity. If they didn't look after their grandchildren, those children would be in foster care or a residential home.

There are believed to be 200,000 grandparents in the UK caring for their grandchildren full time.[1] The children of these grandparents are, for whatever reason, unable to parent their own offspring. It may be that they have serious problems with drug or alcohol abuse.

In such families, if grandparents did not get involved their grandchildren might either be totally neglected or would have to parent their own mother or father.

In the midst of such a challenging situation one might think that a thousand considerations would flood the minds of grandparents, yet in my experience it's a single one which often dominates: guilt. 'Where did we go wrong as parents – *so very wrong* – that our children cannot even care for their own family?' It's understandable, but having spoken to parents across the world in many different cultures I can tell you that guilt is a very common feeling – even amongst parents who have seemingly 'perfect' children. We're dogged by the notion that there must be *something* we could have done better: if we hadn't gone out to work/stayed at home/let them have a television in their bedroom . . . then they would be a hospital consultant by now. One mother wrote to me saying, 'Guilt is an occupational hazard. It comes attached to the placenta.' It's no wonder, then, that the sense of guilt can be even greater for those whose children are not providing good care for their grandchildren.

Whether you are a mother or a father, may I urge you to let that guilt go? Wonderful parents have children who go off the rails. And – which we may find even more annoying – terrible parents have kids who turn out just fine. Most of us have given the task of parenting our very best shot. Have we been perfect parents? No. Do we sometimes long to have another run at it? Yes – but if we could, we would probably just make different mistakes. The truth is that when they reach a certain age our children are responsible for their own choices, and sometimes those are bad ones. The decision to care for grandchildren full time – to stand in the shoes of their parents – is a huge one and not one to be made on the back of a ton of guilt which we may have no reason to carry anyway.

These situations can occur very suddenly. One grandmother was looking after her two grandchildren one Wednesday afternoon while her single-parent daughter was at work. But her daughter didn't come home – ever. She had decided that she couldn't cope as a mother, and left the country with somebody she had met the previous week. Pam and her husband Colin are now almost sixty-five. They put their two grandchildren to bed in their own home on that Wednesday evening and have done so every night for the past ten years.

Those who care for members of their own family – a disabled child, a wheelchair-bound husband, or an elderly parent – are the unsung heroes of our society. They risk being marginalised, unheard and generally taken for granted, despite the fact that they save the state billions of pounds each year. Sometimes grandparents are full-time carers for their grandchildren because the parents have died or are unable to look after them as a result of chronic illness. But whatever the reason, grandparents who act as full-time carers of their grandchildren deserve our admiration. They also deserve the practical support of both society in general and the government – who should be bending over backwards to help them as much as possible (if only because the government have done the maths on the economic and social costs of keeping a child in residential care). Many of these grandparents are in their later years; they have brought up their own children, they have worked all their lives . . . they are tired.

If you are in such a situation now, let me say clearly that however hard it feels, however thankless a task it seems, all the research shows that you are making an incredible difference in the lives of your grandchildren. It doesn't matter if you are not doing a perfect job – the outcomes for your grandchildren, compared with them being in residential or foster care (however good that may be), can be infinitely better. They are safer with you than with anybody else, their lives are more stable with you, and they are less likely to exhibit severe behavioural problems if you are able to care for them in that dedicated way.[2] What you are doing is harder – far harder – than the vast majority of people appreciate, but every day you can do it will make a difference to those kids.

Nonetheless, the day may come when you just can't do it any more – at least on your own. It may be that you need extra help, or some respite care. You will know when that day comes, and once more you will probably have to deal with that demon of guilt. Allow yourself to take the counsel of others – trusted friends, social workers, other family members – as you try to decide the best way to organise ongoing care for your grandchildren.

But let's leave that more unusual situation of full-time care and move on to one that affects millions of grandparents almost every day of their lives.

Providing childcare

Sally was in the kitchen with her daughter, Ruth, and her six-week-old granddaughter, May. She had just put the kettle on and was about to turn round and say, 'A nice cup of tea or coffee?' when Ruth spoke. 'Mum, Carl and I have been talking about when I'll go back to work and we've been looking at some nurseries. They cost an arm and a leg. I wondered whether you'd have May for a couple of hours a day. She'll love it and I bet you will too.'

Sally didn't turn to face her daughter immediately; she just stared at the water pouring into the kettle. She remembered later the dozens of thoughts that rushed through her brain in the seconds before she had to reply to her daughter's request. The first was, 'Oh, no. I just don't think I can do it. I can help out occasionally, of course, but not every day, not regularly – not *always*.'

The second thought that came hard on its heels seemed like it was spoken by an invisible woman at her shoulder. 'How can you be so selfish? You're Ruth's mother. Why wouldn't you help her and Carl? It's so hard for young people today. And anyway, what grand-mother wouldn't want to spend time with her own granddaughter?'

Those were just the first two thoughts! Others came thick and fast: 'I'm too tired', 'I'm just starting to enjoy a little freedom', and deepest and most unnerving of all, 'I'm just not sure I'm up to it. I know I've done it all before, but I don't think I've got the confidence to do it all again.'

But even as these thoughts were whirling through her mind, Sally found herself turning, smiling at her daughter and saying, 'Of course I will, Ruth. Now, would you like one of these chocolate biscuits?' And that's how it began: ten years of childcare – doctors, dentists, gyms, soft play, parks and zoos, tricycles and bicycles, mumps and chickenpox, stewed prunes and grazed knees, 'Wheels On The Bus' and more nappy-changing than she had ever thought possible. It all began with those five little words: 'Of course I will, Ruth.'

Sally is not alone in her task. In the UK over one in three families depend on grandparents for their main form of childcare,[3] which, as I mentioned at the beginning of the book, would cost four *billion* pounds a year if it had to be paid for.[4] And it's not difficult to see why it's needed: the average cost of childcare in the UK is over £5,000 a year,[5] and hiring a nanny costs an eye-watering £25,000 pounds a year.

I know that this is a complicated topic with many nuances, subtexts and a thousand different contexts, but nevertheless I want to suggest four words that any grandparent must consider before taking on regular childcare. They are not relevant in every case, and we have already considered some of the situations where grandparents are not only the best hope of care for their grandchildren but, short of fostering or residential care homes, the *only* hope. With allowances for such exceptions, these four words should be the starting point for any consideration of whether to look after your grandchildren on a regular basis.

I realise these words are so contentious that some of you will write letters to me complaining about them. But on reading them there will be others of you – even if you go on to offer regular childcare for your grandchildren – who will feel as if somebody has removed a ton weight labelled 'Grandparent Guilt' from your shoulders.

Are you ready? Here they are . . .

It's not your responsibility.

Unless we start any consideration of whether we will care for our grandchildren with the message of those four words, we will too easily allow guilt to be our guide. I have met a few media agony aunts, but I never did get to meet Claire Rayner. Someone told me they had listened to her on a radio programme some years ago. A young mum had phoned in to complain that her mother didn't want to care for her granddaughter so that she and her husband could go out on Saturday nights. I don't know whether Claire had eaten breakfast that day or not, but in any event she apparently had a second helping on the radio show that morning. She was livid. 'How dare you criticise your mother for not wanting to look after your children? She's done her job – she's brought you up. Now it's your turn. You are your daughter's parents – *you* look after her!'

As I have said earlier, grandparents can offer wonderful care for their grandchildren and, in doing so, will affect the lives of those children for ever. Many grandparents and their adult children are grateful for the happy coincidence that allows the children to continue to work or study and gives the grandparents the chance to do a task they love. And even when the circumstances are not quite so rosy, many grandparents – while sometimes feeling tired, frustrated and, yes, occasionally a little taken for granted – wouldn't actually change a thing. All that is true, yet taking care of somebody else's children – even if they are your children's children – is not something to be entered into lightly and certainly not with a spontaneous, 'Of course I will. Now how about a chocolate biscuit?'

There is often no 'right' or 'wrong' answer, but providing childcare always has big implications. Maybe you have several adult children – you couldn't possibly provide care for each of your grandchildren. If you say 'yes' to one, then what of the others?

And, of course, although it is true that most childcare is provided by retired grandparents, some grandparents are, themselves, still in paid employment. Of those who are raising their grandchild full time, 35 per cent are reported to go to work[6]. The pressures on them can be even greater. While trying to cope with all of this, we may also be part of the 'sandwich generation' – still trying to help our adult children, but also with responsibilities for ageing parents.

In addition to these, there are a hundred other considerations ranging from 'But I had dreams of what I would do in retirement' to the sentiments expressed by one sixty-one-year-old grandparent: 'Bringing up my own kids as a single parent was so hard, I was looking forward to a rest. I'm just not sure I can gear myself up to doing it all again.' In between these are so many other things to think about: 'I simply don't feel confident enough', perhaps, or, 'I just get too tired.' Whether we end up providing childcare for our grandchildren or not, these are natural concerns to have and it's always best to consider them openly and honestly before taking the plunge.

As I have spoken with grandparents who were involved in their grandchildren's care, time and time again I came upon three questions that they wished they had asked before embarking on the task. That word *before* is very important: this is not a decision to be taken at the drop of a hat. Conditions, boundaries and expectations can all be more easily managed if they are agreed before rather than after we start caring for our grandchildren on a regular basis. It's so much harder to extricate yourself later than to say 'no' (or 'yes, but...') at the beginning. Here are those three questions.

Is it necessary?

Most grandparents are involved in childcare for financial reasons: their children need to work. But we should be sure of that 'need'. It's one thing to care for our grandchildren so that our children can put food on the table, pay their mortgage or rent and generally be able to look after their family. But don't be like the grandmother who, after six years of almost full-time care of her grandson, realised she had been doing it – as she put it – to 'finance a house that was too large, holidays that were too frequent, and plastic surgery that was too obvious'.

Can we start small?

Offer to do a limited amount at first – perhaps something like, 'I could begin with looking after Luke on Tuesday and Wednesday mornings and we'll see how it goes.' It's always easier to be in a position to offer to do some extra hours, or even days, than to have the awkward conversation that starts with the words, 'I'm sorry, but I'm just not coping...'

Another possibility to explore is a compromise between paying professional carers and the help that you are willing to give. Rather than the burden falling on just one set of grandparents, some parents manage to arrange a family rota to cover the childcare. If this is suggested, don't play the martyr; and above all, don't say, 'Oh, it's probably easier if I do it all.' It won't be. But of course the place to start, at least so far as your contribution is concerned, is with asking whether the child's parents can reduce their paid working hours so that they need less childcare. (*Remember the four words*.)

Can we review it in six months?

Stepping into the role of being your grandchild's carer – even if it's part time – can seem such an obvious thing for grandparents to do to help solve their children's childcare problems. But even if you have taken the decision after careful consideration, build in an opportunity to see how it's going. One grandfather put it like this: 'I thought twice about looking after my neighbour's cat for a fortnight while they were in Majorca, and yet I said "yes" to looking after two kids for fifteen years without even thinking about it.'

Other considerations

Of course, there are day-to-day issues to consider, too. The first is relevant whether or not we are carers: 'Is our home grandchild proof?' The list could be quite long, but the obvious points are: keeping medicine and tablets safely away, fitting electrical plugs with covers, fencing off ponds, locking away the contents of garden sheds and cleaning materials, making sure precious objects are out of the reach of little hands, and remembering that the first thing any child under three years old does with any object is to put it in their mouth.

The second can be quite tricky and may only emerge as the childcare goes on. It has to do with discipline. In Chapter 5 we talked about how important it is not to interfere in the way your children discipline their own children when you're not primarily responsible for them. But, having said that, if you're the children's major carer, then at the very least – if only for their own safety – you need some form of discipline that works for you and that your children agree with.

In addition, if your grandchildren are at your house then you have a right to have standards there, even though they may be different from the standards in the children's home – rules about putting feet on the sofa or packing away toys, for example.

I heard of one grandmother who says this to her grandchildren when they forget a rule in her home: 'Now, whose house are you in?'

'Yours, Gran.'

'And who is in charge of this house?'

'You are, Gran.'

'And what does that mean?'

'It means "Grandma's house, Grandma's rules!"'

'Well, let's remember that and then we'll have fun.'

'Yes, Gran.'

She sounds pretty fearsome, doesn't she?

It made me think of the mother who said to her son, 'Why do you do what Granny says more quickly than you do it for me?'

Her son said, 'Because she's sweet.' Then he thought for a bit and added, 'And I don't want her to turn into that thing she sometimes does.'

'What thing?' asked his mother.

'Granimator!'

We have considered the implications of some hard issues that are raised in caring for our grandchildren, but, as one grandparent reminded us, perhaps not *the* hardest. She said that accolade must be reserved for the time when your grandkids' parents come home after you have been looking after them all day and they leave you 'as though you're nothing' and rush into their parents' arms. 'It hurts a bit,' she admitted, 'but I suppose that's how it should be.'

Yes, it is. *But don't expect two bags of sweets next time, you fickle little blighters.*

Sixty Second Page

🕐 Don't rush into long-term childcare.

🕐 Don't agree to childcare out of guilt. You have already done your bit.

🕐 Agree a review date to see how it's working for all parties.

🕐 Make sure your house is a safe place – tablets, plugs, ponds, chemicals, sheds, stairs, etc. If you have pets, be mindful that some animals, especially dogs, can become jealous of babies and small children.

🕐 Aim for consistency. Try to agree a joint policy with your children on rules for television, sweets, bedtimes, discipline.

🕐 Remember you have a right – at least to some extent – to the 'Grandma's House, Grandma's Rules' policy. It's not *all* about what your children want.

🕐 Don't let the amount of childcare creep upwards without considering the extra responsibility and talking it over with your children.

Job Description: Grandparent

- Lifetime position with responsibility for grand-children from birth to beyond maturity.

- To work under supervision of directors of family-oriented organisation that may or may not be anticipating expansion. Not a 9-to-5 job. May involve some travel.

- Higher education not required, previous experience as paediatrician and psychologist helpful. Must have extensive knowledge of human relations.

- Computer experience not necessary – in five years' time grandchild will provide training.

- Skill in reading aloud essential.

- Successful applicant may have multiple duties and functions as required: caregiver, nurturer, play-mate, teacher, spiritual guide, cheerleader.

- Individual must be loving, caring, loving, selfless, loving, accepting and loving.

- Salary: seven figures (£0,000,000) annually. Fringe benefits include overnight accommodation, in addition to generous amounts of hugs and kisses.

- Be-a-Grandparent is an equal-opportunity employer.

Author unknown

7

When a Family is Hurting

This is a sad chapter. I wish with all my heart there were no need to put it in the book. But C.S. Lewis was right when he said, 'To love at all is to be vulnerable. Love anything, and your heart will certainly be wrung and possibly be broken.'[1] A million grandparents in the UK know just *how* right he is. These people are good grandparents, but their children's relationship has broken down and because of that they are suddenly cut off from regular – perhaps from any – contact with the grandchildren they love so much.

Only those who have experienced this trauma can understand what it is: it is no less than grief. Anger? Yes. Confusion? Perhaps. Frustration at the system? Maybe. But above all, the experience is one of soul-destroying grief. One grandparent put it like this: 'We taught her how to build rocky stone castles on the pebbly beach and how to skim stones. In the bedroom she used when she stayed with us, her favourite soft toys, dolls and games are still there waiting for her. We can't bear to put them away. We just hope she will be visiting us regularly again soon.'

Another grandparent says, 'In many ways, we feel like we're grieving. The pain is physical because we miss Kyle and Ellie so much. We already feel we've missed out on so much of their little lives. These grand-children are our flesh and blood and our life is empty without them. Whatever went wrong between Louise and our son isn't our fault or the children's – and yet we are all being punished.'

Time and time again grandparents say, 'What can we do about this? It can't be right or good for our grand-children that suddenly we're not allowed to see them any more. We don't want to interfere in our children's lives, but please help us see them again.'

For grandparents who are experiencing this trauma and desperately want to re-establish contact with their grandchildren there are two routes that are available. But even where neither of those routes is successful there are some strategies that, while not taking the pain away now, will almost certainly be in the interests of both grand-children and grandparents over the long haul.

The first of those two routes is by way of the legal system – through the courts. The second is relational – through discussions with family members, often with a daughter-in-law.

Sadly, the route by way of the legal system is a very difficult one for grandparents. In the UK grandparents do not have automatic visitation rights with their grandchildren. This is the case even when, because of childcare arrangements, the grandparents may have had more daily contact with the child than the parents. Grandparents can, however, ask the court to grant them visitation rights – this is called a 'contact order'. To be successful in this they have to prove that such contact would have a positive influence on the child and that allowing the parents to exclude them from their grandchild's life would harm the child in some way. The process is fraught, however, without any guarantee of success. At the back of this book are the names of some organisations that can offer advice in this area.

The second route to re-establishing contact with a grandchild is through discussion with the child's parents. The most common situation is that a daughter-in-law does not want her children to have regular contact with her former partner's parents. But whoever has custody of the children, we need to approach them and say that whatever the problems between the adults, we just want to be good grandparents – without taking sides. We want to be there to offer some love and stability for the grandchildren, especially if they have been through an unsettling time.

The truth is that after their relationship has broken down, one of the most significant factors that will decide whether a parent wishes their child to have ongoing access to a grandparent is the quality of relationship they had with that grandparent *before* the split. If we have always taken sides with our own child in any dispute with their partner, or been negative or unwelcoming towards that partner, then our relationship with our son- or daughter-in-law is likely to be strained after the breakdown. They can often feel that we blame them for the problem, and may perhaps fear that if the grandchildren are allowed to visit us we will poison their minds against them.

If, on the other hand, we have always been seen as even handed during the marriage, and have been loving and welcoming to our son- or daughter-in-law, they will have less to fear from an ongoing relationship with us. However, a small warning: when couple relationships break down, it is often such a time of trauma, blame and counter-blame that perfectly good grandparents get caught in the crossfire *anyway*.

Of course, what we are considering here is only the end-game of a relationship breakdown that may have been developing over many years. What can a grandparent do as they watch their child's relationship deteriorate? Well, as we have already said, the best thing is, as far as possible, to maintain an even-handedness between the parties. But perhaps the area in which we can be of most help is in giving emotional support to our grandchildren.

The effect on children of observing the breakdown of their parents' relationship is often traumatic. Sometimes the children may believe that the breakdown is somehow their fault. A common response is, 'What did I do to make Mum and Dad not love each other any more?' But even if they don't feel that sense of guilt, they will undoubtedly feel unease, uncertainty and instability. One ten-year-old whose father had just left his mother put it like this. Sitting on a step outside his house, he looked up and said, 'My father doesn't love my mother any more and he has left us now.' And then this child shrugged his shoulders and said, 'What can a kid do?'

At such a time – when a child's very foundations are shaken – a grandparent can be a rock. One single-parent mum said: 'Since Matt left, my dad has been the main male role model in my son's life and I am so grateful for him.' Research from Oxford University found that a close relationship between grandparents and grand-children can act as a 'buffer' against the adverse effects of some life events, such as parental separation.[2] It's not surprising. In a world where everything seems to have shifted, grandparents can give a sense of stability. At these times the simple repetition of the traditions that always go on at 'Grandma's house' – stories, treats, games, reading and fun – can help steady a young life that is rocking at that moment.

Be there for your grandchildren

But there is a potential danger even in the security of 'Grandma's house': be careful what you say in front of them. You may well have strong views, but don't let them hear you taking sides with one of their parents against another. The problem with little ones is often not so much that they don't listen, but that not a word they hear is lost. It may not be obvious at the time, but they take it all in. Try to develop two skills for which grandparents are justly renowned. First, give the incredible gift of somebody who has time to just . . . *listen.* And second, remember that even in times of pain children need to laugh. At home things will almost certainly be tense and difficult, but whether they are five or fifteen, if you can bring out a smile with either a tickle or a tenner, you will have done well.

Finally, let's just return for a moment to that situation where contact with our grandchildren is not possible. Although it is so painful that, as we have said, we feel grief, remember that it is not death. These children are alive and growing. Therefore we must *do what we can.* Our task here is to consider the long haul – to look forward to the day when those children will be able to make their own decision on what kind of grandparent we were. This will encourage us to sow seeds now for a future harvest. Stay in touch in any way that is appropriate; keep sending birthday cards and presents – even if you are unsure they will get through. Let those grandchildren know that you still love them.

Sometimes even the most desperate situations turn out better than we had dared hope. I think of Anthony and Maureen, two grandparents who, through no fault of their own, were denied any further contact at all with the seven-year-old boy whom they had practically brought up before his parents split. They had not heard from him for over eleven years, but they had never missed sending him a birthday or Christmas present, always sent a card before examinations were due, and in between had written as many letters as they felt appropriate to send – although none were acknowledged.

It was five o'clock on a winter's evening when Anthony's and Maureen's doorbell sounded. Anthony told his wife that he would get it, eased himself out of the armchair and walked towards the door. He later said that the second he saw the shape behind the glass, he knew. There was no reason why he should have known so quickly, for the young man standing there was, in many ways, quite different from when Anthony had last seen him. Yet as Anthony opened the door and listened to what the man said, the years seemed to roll away. 'Hey, Gramps! Tell Nan to get my favourite cake in the oven . . .'

Sixty Second Page

🕐 In tough times a grandparent's home can be a refuge. Make allowances for your grandchildren – they may well be hurting deeply.

🕐 Keep doing the old things with them – games, stories, visits. It will bring a little stability.

🕐 Have fun – make your grandchildren laugh. And remember that 'boring' is far worse than 'batty'.

🕐 Don't speak negatively about either of their parents to your grandchildren. And remember, they are *always* listening.

🕐 Don't ply them for information on what life is like at home – just be ready if they need to talk about it.

🕐 As far as possible, try to have good relations with both your grandchildren's parents – even if you have to bite your tongue once in a while.

'Grandpa, will you make a noise like a frog?'

'No. Now, what shall we play today?'

'Grandpa, please make a noise like a frog.'

'I've already said "no". Now, shall we have a game of football?'

'Grandpa [floods of tears], please, please, please make a noise like a frog!'

'Why on earth do you want me to make a noise like a frog?'

'Because Daddy says, when you croak we can all go to Disney World.'

8

From a Distance

Celia was in the kitchen when the phone rang. It was her daughter, Megan. 'Mum, great news! Jack has got the job! He starts in September.'

Celia remembers saying, 'Oh, my love, that's wonderful! Really wonderful news. Give him a big kiss from me.' She doesn't recall saying much else, although she knows the conversation went on for at least twenty minutes. What she *does* remember is the same thought going over and over in her mind: 'But the job is in Manchester. That's 180 miles away. What about the grandchildren? How will we see them?' She only just stopped herself from saying, 'But what about the kids? What about *us*?'

Over the next few months Celia cried a lot – oh, but not so anybody could see. It was as if she felt a huge knot in her stomach and the silly thing was, she couldn't really explain it. After all, she told herself, she had so much to be grateful for. Her daughter was happily married and had a toddler and a new baby. They were only moving to Manchester, not Mumbai, and so many grandparents had to face so much worse. So why did she feel like this?

The truth was that, as in the case of grandparents who are not allowed access to their grandchildren, Celia was experiencing grief. Grief is not something that only attaches itself to death, but it also applies to the loss of the presence – even temporarily – of somebody (or even *something*) that we love dearly.

Steve's and Gill's son, Rhys, and his wife, Jenny, live in California. A couple of years ago Rhys emailed his dad to make sure he set Skype up for seven o'clock that evening. Try as he might, Steve couldn't get it working and sent a quick email to Rhys: 'Sorry, we'll have to try again tomorrow.'

The reply came back immediately. 'No, keep trying. We *have* to speak with you now.'

Steve said that Gill immediately went into her 'What if . . . ?' routine: 'What if one of them is ill? What if Rhys has lost his job?' And then she looked up at Steve and said, 'What if Jenny is pregnant?'

Apparently even the gremlins that afflict Skype had some compassion and sure enough, Steve and Rhys eventually hooked up. The second Gill saw her son's face on the computer screen she knew she had nothing to fear, and pretty soon Rhys – with a smile that brought to mind cats and cream – shared the news. He was going to be a dad.

Gill says she remembers this incredible sense of joy surging through her body. She and Steve had not been able to have children of their own – both Rhys and his brother Owain were adopted. She felt as happy as she can ever remember being, and then suddenly she sensed a deep pang in her heart. When she described it later she said, 'It was as if I was separated – by far too many miles – from this little one now growing in Jenny's womb. In an instant, I already loved this child and I wanted to be with him or her not just now, but always.' She turned to Steve and said, 'We're going to be grand-parents. How do you grandparent across an ocean?'

We may not be separated by an ocean, but many grandparents live hundreds of miles from their children. How can such grandparents still be involved in the lives of their grandchildren? How can they make the very best of that situation? How do they grandparent at a distance?

At first sight the task can seem daunting. The old proverb sums up the heart of the problem: 'Out of sight, out of mind.' Because of this, couples facing years apart – perhaps because of war or a dozen other reasons – have been advised, 'End it. Find somebody else in another place or in another time.' Such counsel is hard to argue against, for time together is almost always necessary for a relationship to be sustained. But it's not the whole story: many could testify that against all the odds there is another way – and other outcomes. There are occasions where the love is so deep and the commitment so great that the relationship at a distance hem that nobody said on their deathbed, 'I wish I'd pent more time at the office.' But sometimes it's not hat straightforward. If they are to put bread on the able, some of those fathers have to be away from home a lot. In such circumstances those who keep a strong relationship with their children find ways to sustain that relationship in spite of the physical separation. I remember a long-distance lorry driver saying to me, 'When you have to be away from home you have to work harder at relationships. I let my children know in a dozen ways I'd rather be with them. And when I'm home, I let *nothing* rob me of that time with them. They get my undivided attention. When I get home I don't want them thinking about whether I have bought them large presents; I want them to be excited about seeing *me*.'

I have often thought about that father and I have come to believe that children can more easily handle a father who they know has to be away a lot but would rather be with them, than they can a father who, though he is physically present in the house, is constantly somewhere else in his heart and mind.

I believe that lorry driver's story should be a wonderful comfort and encouragement to those who grandparent at a distance, for it holds within it some of the secrets to building relationships when one of the normal ingredients is missing: *time*. Like lovers who have to sustain their relationship through the long years of a war, they learn lessons that can make them not only effective grandparents, but sometimes even more effective than grandparents who live near their children.

not only survives, but *thrives*. Critics of such l
ask how their relationships can possibly su
alone blossom; to those critics, the lovers s
quote another proverb, 'Absence makes the he
fonder.'

Keeping in touch

Building strong relationships at a distance is
but there's no doubt that it definitely takes mo
One grandfather said, 'The phone is importa
I've got a call plan that allows me to ring
numbers free of charge for as long as I like – an
I make use of it. I know when they're teenag
probably won't want to speak to me so much,
now I'm loving it. When they tell me things l
friends' or teachers' names, I make a note of th
when we next speak I say, "And how is Miss
doing?" They are amazed that their old grand
such a brilliant memory!'

A grandmother says, 'When I ring, I make s
the grandchildren know it's for them especially.
spend an age talking to my children or get the
passed around the whole family. I want Emily a
to feel that when I ring to speak to them, it's
Having said that, these days you have to compe
the telly or a computer game, so I've learnt nc
hurt when I hear, "Got to go now, Nan."'

Over the years I have spoken to thousands
about the role of fatherhood. I have urged them to
as much time as possible with their children, ren

Do you recall that when you were a child, time seemed to move more slowly? And isn't it strange that the things you now remember are not those you spent most time doing – like sitting in class – but those that, although not time intensive, made you feel *special*. The most successful grandparents from a distance have learnt the secrets that help their grandchildren feel as if they matter to them more than anybody else on the face of the earth – irrespective of the time spent with them.

Those secrets are not complicated. They have to do with consistency:

'My Granddad always rings me on a Monday night.'
'My Nan sends me a letter every Friday.'
'My Grampy never forgets my birthday.'

And they have to do with traditions:

'When I go to visit Gran in the summer holidays she makes a big tent out of the sheets on the bed and we tell stories in it and eat chocolate.'
'Pops and I always sing "Bring Me Sunshine" together when we finish talking on the phone.'

I know one grandfather who has managed to teach his three-year-old grandson to sing 'The Gambler' word perfect. Apparently his daughter is not enamoured of hearing her son on the phone to the old boy gleefully singing, 'You've got to know when to hold 'em, know when to fold 'em.'

Those who are young remember the things we do over and over again with them, even though the actual time spent on them is small. One grandfather bought two copies of a child's storybook and sent one to his grandson. Once a week they read their special book over the phone *together*. Another grandfather makes recordings – and occasionally videos – of himself reading favourite stories and his granddaughter listens to them before going to sleep.

The truth is that sometimes making a child feel special can be a little easier when we grandparent at a distance. Such grandparents have not seen the new dance a dozen times already, watched *Monsters Inc.* thirty-three times, or had to read the same story over and over again. The grandchildren of such grandparents have an audience that genuinely wants to see the same show again.

Of course, it's also true that with modern technology the task of grandparenting at a distance is easier than ever. Those who are separated by the miles from their grandchildren sometimes have more interaction with them than those who live nearby. I think now of a grandfather who describes himself as a technophobe, but has become a regular Skype user because, as he put it, 'I realised if I wanted to be part of my grandchildren's everyday lives then I had better pull my finger out and get with it.' For the very same reason, many grandparents who still can't programme the central heating are adept at email, Twitter and Facebook, and can even be found battling it out with their grandchildren in interactive games over the Internet.

Visits

Grandparenting at a distance, however, is not just about phones, letters and leading-edge technology; there comes the time when we can actually be with our grandchildren. If this occasion was a film, it would simply be called *The Visit* and, like all good films, it would have some joy in it – and the potential for tragedy.

One of the greatest difficulties with a visit either to or from grandchildren is the same gremlin that has laid low many a family get-together at Christmas – our high expectations. It may be that, having travelled nearly three hundred miles, we are disappointed to discover that actually the grandchildren are more interested in watching *EastEnders* than spending time with us. But, of course, they have their own lives and interests just as we do, and children are often more honest in letting us know it. It's the same if they visit us. The most important thing is not that they spend every waking moment with us, but that they really enjoy the visit and want to come back. Especially with older children, it's as well to acknowledge from the outset that they are unlikely to want to spend hours chatting on the settee 'catching up'. Doing some research and a recce before they come to find out what activities they would *love* to do is a really good idea.

If children are very young and visits infrequent, it's always worth doing some spadework first. Some couples put pictures of their parents on low shelves or cabinets so that their small children can get used to what their grandparents look like. Other couples ask their parents to make scrapbooks about themselves – where they used to live, work, and how they met each other. The idea is that by the time the grandparents visit, the grandchildren feel as if they know them – if only just a little.

Letters, Skype, email, Facebook, treats, traditions, phones and stories – there are many ways to keep and build relationships at a distance, but my favourite by far is a little idea devised by a grandmother for her small granddaughter. She made a brightly coloured wrap that had an outline of her own hands at either end. She told her granddaughter that at any time she could ask her mum to curl it around her and she would feel her nan's arms hugging her. She had no idea how important the present would become to a very insistent two-year-old. Every night, just as her grandmother in Scotland is waking up, a small child in Sydney, Australia falls off to sleep with her nan's 'arms' wrapped tightly around her.

When we grandparent at a distance we can face many difficulties, but the rewards can be great – for grandparent and grandchild alike. One child put it like this: 'My grandmother really loves me. Even though I live hundreds of miles away from her, I talk to her almost every day. Sometimes she sends me stamps for my collection and she sends me jokes on my mobile. Every year I spend a week with her and we have such a laugh. I think when I'm older I would like to live near my gran.'

The message to those who grandparent at a distance is this: you can have a strong relationship with your grandchildren. You can foster love and deep relationships. You can pass on values and encouragement. In fact, you can often build a stronger relationship than those whose access to grandchildren is so much easier. There is no doubt that it's harder to grandparent at a distance – and perhaps, therefore, we have to try harder than those for whom it's not an issue. But the great encouragement, of which we should never lose sight, is this:

Love travels well.

Sixty Second Page

🕐 If you haven't already, take the plunge and learn how to email and use Skype.

🕐 Start an episodic story through letters or email. You write the first paragraph, send it to your grandchild, they write the next paragraph and send it back to you, and so on.

🕐 Buy a box of chocolates and put a short message under each chocolate. Send it to your grandchild and tell them they are allowed one chocolate a day.

🕐 Organise a long-distance treasure hunt. Send small treats to your grandchild's parents and ask them to hide them one by one. Give your grandchild clues over the phone or by email.

🕐 Remember that even in a technological age, children love getting things through the post – letters, postcards, little surprises.

🕐 Create scrapbooks of your visits – photographs, tickets, brochures, stories. Make sure you capture those memories to share later.

My granddaughter came to spend a few weeks with me, and I decided to teach her to knit. She watched me solemnly, mouth open, as I cast on and knitted the first few rows in stocking stitch. I was rather pleased at the impression I was making, and decided to show off a bit by creating a fancy pattern. My granddaughter seemed to be enthralled, watching carefully and examining the knitting as it grew. Encouraged by her obvious interest, I showed her a Fair Isle jumper I had made, with its intricate and colourful patterns.

Suddenly she stood up, put her hands on her hips and shook her head disbelievingly: 'Nanna, you mean you can do all that, but you can't play my Game Boy?'

9

Bonus Grandchildren

Charles and Emily remember very clearly the day that their daughter Claire told them that she was getting married to Phil. Phil had been divorced five years earlier and had two children aged five and thirteen – Ethan and Chloe. Charles and Emily were already grandparents of three children from Claire's previous marriage – Beccy, Eva and Sam – and because Claire had been a single parent for seven years they were very involved in those children's lives, and very close to them. That night, as Emily was getting into bed, Charles suddenly raised a subject that Emily guessed he had been chewing over since Claire had shared her news: 'I'm sure we'll get on fine with Phil, but what is it going to be like having two new grandchildren that we don't even know – let alone love?'

Charles's concerns are understandable, but I wonder

if he realised that the two prospective step-grandchildren may also have had worries about the same situation. Every blended family begins with more challenges than other families because, by its very nature, it is born of loss – a bereavement, a divorce or a separation. Emotions can be very raw, and although the new husband and wife may be quite certain about the way ahead, other members of the family – and especially their children – can be much more wary; after all, they have lost somebody whom they probably still love dearly. They are already dealing with the challenge of accepting a new 'Mum' or 'Dad', and they have to cope with step-*grand*parents whom they may have hardly met. One teenager put it like this: 'I'm learning to get used to a new house, a new mother, three new brothers, a dog and a rabbit. That's quite enough for one kid without having to kiss some new grandmother.'

I wonder how Charles, Emily and their new step-grandchildren will get on in the future. What does life hold for them? Perhaps they have an advantage because, although worried about the relationship, they are at least talking about it. And if they are wise, they will go on doing so – not just to each other but to others who have already been along this road.

It may be that in one of those conversations a friend will tackle head on the issue which almost certainly lay behind the question that Charles asked his wife as they got into bed that night: 'Can we ever love Ethan and Chloe as much as our "natural" grandchildren?' It may be a relief and a help if that friend tells them honestly that they can't – at least, not for a long time.

But what may be a greater help is if Charles can grasp that genuine love – whether for a friend, husband, wife or child – is not just about feelings but about actually 'doing things': *love in action*. In this respect, both Charles and Emily can make a firm decision that they will love their step-grandchildren in attitude and actions every bit as much as the children to whom they are blood-related. As far as the outside world can tell, each grandchild – step- or otherwise – will be treated exactly the same. They will try to get to everyone's school concert, they will praise all of them equally, they will treat each the same. They can't change the very special feelings they have for Eva, Beccy and Sam, but they can make sure that on birthdays Sam doesn't get a bike and Ethan a plastic trumpet.

If they are to succeed as step-grandparents, Charles and Emily will have to try hard to get to know Ethan and Chloe and build a relationship with them as *individuals*. The truth is that the younger the children are, the easier this is to achieve, with babies being the easiest of all. With older children it's harder; after all, you are strangers to them and you have not had the experience of seeing them grow and develop. For this very reason Charles and Emily should be realistic about their chances of quick success with Chloe, aged thirteen. Here, it has to be said, they may have an uphill battle, possibly for quite a while. They are becoming step-grandparents at the very moment when Chloe is reaching a stage of life during which she may suddenly be uncooperative, unfeeling and generally rude – not just to them, but to any adult in sight. It's quite possible that during this period her mother will feel she is the worst parent on the face of the earth, her teachers will consider becoming accountants, but her friends will think she's the best thing since sliced bread. The key phrase here is, 'Do what you can.' Don't expect too much, try to be a friend, and above all don't take it personally.

Perhaps we should also remember that some step-grandchildren will be very wary of making new relationships. They may still be feeling let down over the ones that have broken, and may worry that their loyalties are being tested. It may be that Ethan and Chloe will feel that in being nice, or even polite, to Charles and Emily they are being disloyal to their other four 'real' grandparents – and indeed their mother. In these circumstances we need to focus not on *our* wishes for the relationship, but on the needs of each child, for although it can be very hard, step-grandparents can have a wonderful healing role in families. If we are prepared at first simply to be a new friend to a child, we may well become not only part of the healing process, but also, while that process is happening, a refuge.

The truth is that Ethan and Chloe might be trying hard to be part of Charles's and Emily's life – just as Charles and Emily are trying hard to be part of theirs. But it's more difficult when you're a child. They know they have to have some kind of relationship with the step-grandparents, they just aren't sure how that's supposed to work. They understand that they are in a different category to the 'natural' grandchildren, but what will really help them is to feel that they are given dignity as individuals. This means that Charles and Emily will be prepared to listen to them, to try to discover what makes them tick, to take time helping them to get to know their new step-grandparents, and to share with them a little of the history of their own family.

To show such care and 'love in action' may be very difficult. We may blame the step-grandchild's other parent for the break-up of our own child's marriage, but even if we do we would be wise to tread carefully, for whatever the truth, it is not the grandchild's fault. It is normally best to steer well away from forays into the past and discussions as to who bears most blame – certainly in front of the child. Remember what I mentioned earlier: the problem with children is often not that they don't listen to us, but that not a word we say is lost. And if we can take it, any step towards a stronger relationship with our new daughter- or son-in-law will inevitably make the relationship with our step-grandchild easier.

As I mentioned earlier, grandparenting is not, primarily, 'about us'. When we become step-grandparents, in particular, we will do well to focus on the needs of the children. One grandfather put it like this: 'We made the mistake of rushing things with the step-grandchildren partly because we were so keen to have a close relationship. What we hadn't realised was that they had a strong bond with the parents of their dad, who has now remarried, and in some ways there didn't seem to be any room for us. Then we decided to back off a little and take things more slowly. We let the children know that we are interested in them and are available to visit and do things with them whenever the possibility arises. We have learnt not to resent the relationships our step-grandchildren have with others and to enjoy the relationship we do have.'

It's true that step-family relationships can be complicated; there may be a lot of different individuals involved, with very different life histories and loyalties, and often with accompanying hurts. Perhaps more than with any other grandparenting relationship, this is one that may take years – even decades – to develop.

But let the last word on the issue go to step-mother and step-grandmother Miriam Stoppard: 'I think I learnt hard lessons when I became the step-mother of two little boys. It was very hard and I often felt emotionally bruised – until I lowered my sights and decided a better approach was simply to try to be their friend.'

Sixty Second Page

🕐 Be prepared to take it gradually. A relationship between a child and a new step-grandparent is like any other – it takes time to build trust.

🕐 Acknowledge to yourself that it's normal to feel closer to your natural grandchildren, but do your very best not to show favouritism.

🕐 Spend as much time as you can with each of your grandchildren one to one. If possible, create times when they don't have to compete for attention.

🕐 Remember *all* your grandchildren's birthdays or special events.

🕐 Don't rely on expensive presents or treats to win over your step-grandchildren. Try to be a friend to them.

🕐 You're the adult; make allowances for the emotions of your step-grandchild – perhaps insecurity, sadness, resentment, jealousy. Go as easy as possible on them.

After putting her small grandchildren to bed, Gran slipped into old trousers and a huge, droopy, stained T-shirt and proceeded to wash her hair.

The children started talking and playing in the dark and after several shouted attempts to quieten them, she finally lost patience. She wrapped a towel around her head and stormed into their room, putting them back to bed with stern warnings. As she left the room, she heard the three-year-old say with a trembling voice, 'Who was *that*?'

10

A Story of Grandparenting

While I was writing *The Sixty Minute Grandparent* I met up with Rob and Marion White. They told me something of their experience of being grandparents and the second they did I knew I wanted to share it with you. Here is their story.

I suppose before we have grandchildren we all imagine what it will be like if they ever come along. We might have images of taking them to the beach, chasing them in the park, or being the first one to show them a lion in the zoo. I used to have those images as well – and in every one of them the sun was shining: life was perfect. But sometimes life doesn't turn out as we imagine it will.

I remember very clearly when we heard we were going to be grandparents. It was the wedding day of one of our twin daughters, but it was the other twin, Jo, who told us she thought she was pregnant. It came as a huge shock to us. She was mid-way through a college course and her pregnancy was certainly not planned. Somehow the reality of our becoming grandparents was not at all the way we'd imagined it would be.

Some difficult times ensued and some hard decisions had to be taken, but in due time Adora-Beth – meaning 'adored and precious gift' – was born. Our daughter and Dorrie, as she came to be called, lived with us for the first few months and this new little baby was truly loved and adored from the moment she was born.

Our first grandchild didn't arrive into a neat and tidy family. Her parents' relationship didn't continue, and Dorrie's father didn't have any contact with her for the first four years of her life, but once he met her he was truly smitten. He has been committed to her ever since, seeing her on a regular basis and being a good support to her.

Because of all the ups and downs that surrounded Dorrie's arrival she has always been, and always will be, incredibly special to us. She lived close by for the first seven years of her life and we were very involved practically in supporting her, and our daughter as a single parent. My husband willingly took on not only the role of grandfather, but in some ways of dad as well.

Being a granny in this situation was not always easy, and I soon realised that I had to allow my daughter to be the mum that Dorrie needed and try not to interfere. This is not easy for any grandparent, but especially in a situation such as this, and I didn't always manage it well! And yet, as I let go, I began to see that my daughter had skills as a mum that I never had when my children were small. She married when Dorrie was seven and moved some distance away from us. Of course we were happy for her; of course we knew that she needed to establish her life with her new husband; and of course we felt the loss when Dorrie was no longer living nearby.

Our second grandchild was born to our other twin daughter, Deborah. Josh was such a beautiful baby and so contented – maybe a bit too passive. Just before his first birthday he started having very bad fits. It was when he was in hospital after one of these fits that he was diagnosed with epilepsy and cerebral atrophy, but it was not until he was ten that he was diagnosed with cerebral palsy. Josh is now nineteen and is wheelchair-bound with no mobility in his legs at all.

I'd like to especially encourage any grandparent who has a grandchild with special needs or learning difficulties, because your role becomes critical. As well as them often needing your physical and practical help, giving emotional support to the parents is vital. It is not possible to take away their pain at not having a healthy child, but they do need us to be alongside them and to try to understand some of the huge difficulties. As Josh's grand-parent I have often felt helpless to really understand how my daughter feels, but have been able to give practical help, particularly accessing the right help and support from all the varied service providers.

When Josh was little he picked up an amazing range of swear words which he used when he was frustrated or just because he didn't understand what he was saying. Our daughter would some-times go to the supermarket with him and end up leaving her trolley and walking out in tears because other people would look askance at her for not controlling him better. Because I could be more detached, I was quite happy to take him shopping, and could cope with these situations without becoming upset and swearing as well (that is, if you don't count that tiny naughty word that I uttered just once at a 'supermum' in the freezer section of Asda's).

We take Josh out for his tea once a week and he chooses where he would like to go. He likes trying to help me do crosswords, and the challenge is to make the clues easier so that he can guess correctly.

I remember when we heard that Dorrie, who was now eight, was to have a brother, our second grandson, Isaac. We were full of joy, although after he was born that joy was tinged with sadness as we soon realised that, like his cousin, he too has special needs. He also was eventually diagnosed with cerebral palsy. The jury is out as to whether it is a genetic flaw, a result of our daughters being identical twins, or something entirely different.

I have to say that my husband and I have found grandparenting in these situations very challenging, and it has caused us many times to ask the question, 'Why?' There are no easy answers to what life brings, and I realise that different people believe different things, but we have found strength and comfort in being able to pray together and to believe that God loves each of our grandchildren in exactly the same way. As a family we have a much greater awareness of those with special needs, we appreciate the depth of love and care that our grandsons bring us, and we are drawn together through our experiences over these years.

We have three other granddaughters, Mia and Amelie (the children of our other daughter, Naomi) and Gabriella (Jo's youngest). Of course we love all our grandchildren to bits – they each bring us such joy – but it is fair to say that I have found being a grandmother both exhilarating and utterly exhausting. We helped our children with childcare on a regular basis, and I have to confess there have been times when I did not make a complete success of this. Once, walking home from the shops with twenty-month-old Amelie, I lost her – her parents had omitted to warn me that she was going through a stage of making a bid for freedom and running off at great speed! After about ten minutes of searching in sheer panic, with her big sister Mia making comments like, 'Mummy and Daddy will be very cross if you have lost Amelie,' we were eventually reunited. I did offer to step down from my weekly day of childcare, but my daughter informed me that however much of a liability I might be, they couldn't afford anyone else!

And while I'm at it, I may as well admit to an incident when I must have dozed off momentarily while watching CBeebies with Mia and she some-how got hold of the phone and managed to dial 999. The first I knew of this was when a police-man knocked at the door, wanting to know if we were all right!

I found Rob's and Marion's story extremely moving. When a child is born with special needs or disabilities it is, of course, natural that our thoughts go to the parents. Nevertheless, the child's grandparents will experience many of the same feelings as the parents – perhaps sadness, grief, shock, denial and, finally, acceptance. And, of course, just at the time when their children need their support more than ever, they themselves will also be coping with all those emotions. Even as I write, my mind goes to a grandmother in exactly that situa-tion who has tirelessly supported her daughter and her severely challenged son. People say to her, 'You're so strong.' Yes, she is; but they have no knowledge of the tears she has cried in secret.

Sometimes, though, it's simply not possible to give all the support we would wish to, and – particularly for grandparents who live at a distance – this can lead to feelings of understandable but irrational guilt. Grandparents in this situation have another challenge to face: it can be easy for them to hear only of the difficulties, the bad times, whereas those who are in regular contact with a disabled grandchild often have the privilege of seeing first hand the more positive things – small milestones reached, little achievements and, most of all, the child's own character emerging, in spite of the disability. It's so important in that situation that as well as sharing the pain they may be going through, the parents also share any encouragements in their child's life, however small, *even just a smile*.

Marion's story demonstrates the vital role that vast numbers of grandparents play in supporting their children and grandchildren every day, both practically and emotionally. Perhaps the most important gift grandparents can give to both their children and grandchildren is their unconditional love and acceptance. They may need to support the new parents through a journey that can include worry, stress, guilt and fear about caring for their special needs child.

Some of the principles we have looked at earlier are just as, or even more, important here. Our loving support must be given in tandem with respect for the role of the parents; and it is far better to ask our children how we can be of help than to assume a task that they may not wish us to undertake. That said, our contribution can be very significant both in emotional support and practical help: we can learn as much as possible about our grandchild's condition, we can let our children know that we are interested in hearing about or reading all the information they receive from professionals; we can offer to accompany them to doctors' appointments and help in a myriad other ways. Of course, the level of support we are able to give will depend on our own circumstances and abilities, but our willingness to understand, listen and learn about the challenges, and to give the help that we can, will be a support to the whole family that no other agency can bring, no matter how efficient it may be.

As this chapter comes to a close, let's give Marion the last word:

> I hope a little of our story will help encourage any grandparent who is trying to do their best in very difficult circumstances – even if different from ours. We can't be 'perfect' grandparents – I gave up the burden of trying to be that long ago. But we can give this task – and privilege – our very best effort. And if you ever feel really rubbish at it, then remember that there is at least one very imperfect grandparent out there who loses her children's children and has the police knocking on the door just to check if everything is all right!

11

The Secret

In *The Sixty Minute Grandparent* we have met all kinds of grandparents – sky-diving grannies, pipe-and-slippers granddads, ready-to-go nanas and dodgy-song-teaching poppas. We have looked at many of the joys and challenges of this incredible role, from getting the news of the pregnancy to that most dangerous of high-wire acts, finding the balance between helping and interfering. But as we come to a close, there is one particular grandfather who comes to my mind. Perhaps he does so because we have just read Rob's and Marion's story, but he symbolises for me what I believe should be the ultimate goal of every grandparent and is certainly the greatest need of every child: to give and receive unconditional love.

Some time ago, a friend of mine attended a school prize-giving, but one with a difference. This school cared for severely physically and mentally disadvantaged children. The audience listened as the head read out the children's names and the reasons why these particular pupils had won a prize. 'Mark, because he has fed himself all this term', 'Richard, because he has learnt to wipe his bottom', and 'Susan, who has recited a poem and can brush her teeth'. As some shuffled and others danced to collect their trophies, there was hardly a dry eye in the place.

The last child to go up to the rostrum had Down's syndrome as well as other physical challenges. The head read out the accreditation: 'Finally, a prize for Peter Harries – who is awarded most improved pupil of the year.' Peter was wheeled down the aisle towards the podium with his hands above his head in the traditional athlete's signal of triumph. As he reached the ramp at the foot of the podium a man sitting next to my friend suddenly stood up and started cheering at the top of his voice. The audience responded in kind and by the time Peter reached the head teacher the place was going crazy. Finally the prize was presented and the noise abated. As he sat down, the man next to my friend whispered to him, 'He's my grandson.'

For all of us life can be testing, but what an asset that sort of grandparent will be in facing it. That is, perhaps, why one child said, 'A grandfather is a little bit parent, a little bit teacher, and a little bit best friend.'

The truth is that most of us – even as adults – crave for somebody who looks for the best in us: someone to whom praise comes more quickly than criticism. An elderly grandmother went to watch her grandson at the school sports day. Tom didn't get into the final of the 100 metres or the 200 metres, and he was unplaced in the longer races as well. In fact, the only event in which he looked remotely comfortable was the egg-and-spoon race, but even then he came last. As Tom and his grandmother walked away together, the little boy's head was down until she put her arm around him and whispered, 'You were the only one whose egg didn't fall off the spoon.' That young boy never did make it as a sportsman, but against the odds he did achieve great things in other areas of his life. I'm not surprised: it's hard to fail with a grandmother like that.

Imagine having somebody who could make you feel that special. Somebody who, when you were three, would 'eat' with relish the plastic sausages you cooked for dinner, and when you were thirteen and discovered your first zit, both understood how important that was and yet made you feel it was practically invisible. Imagine somebody who had so much time and loved you so much that they listened for weeks on end to the story of your first love affair, and made you hot chocolate when it ended. Imagine somebody with time to pass on traditions and values. Somebody who, when you are grown and perhaps have been written off by almost everybody else, took time to write to you, to ring you – even, perhaps, to pray for you.

When grandparenting works best, it does so as a support to both parents and children. Free of the daily routines, discipline issues and major responsibilities, grandparents can more easily make a child feel special. One small child said, 'Grandmas don't just say, "That's nice." They roll their eyes and throw up their hands and smile big! You get your money's worth out of grandmas.'

Yes, you get your money's worth out of grandparents. I know it's not all plain sailing. Author Gene Perrot said, 'An hour with your grandchildren can make you feel young again. Anything longer than that and you start to age quickly.' He's right: grandparenting can bring with it many challenges and we've considered some of them together. And yet for many grandparents there is a reward that, if we are wise, we will keep as a secret from our children. To them we are responsible older people who lavish love and care on their darling offspring because we are such wonderful, selfless people. But what we hope they never realise is that for some of us the reason is much simpler . . .

Grandparents get to play again.

Notes

Chapter 1

1 S. Dex and H. Joshi, *Millennium Cohort Study* (Institute of Education, 2004).

2 *The Economy of Older People* (Age Concern, 2004).

3 *Northern Ireland Life and Times Survey* 2004, Module: Grandparenting and Family Life.

Chapter 2

1 Rick Warren, *The Purpose Driven Life* (Zondervan, 2007).

Chapter 3

1 http://parenthood.library.wisc.edu/Westman/ Westman-Grandparenthood.html.

2 ibid.

Chapter 4

1 Professional Educators Benefits Company, http:// www.pebco.org/page5.htm.

2 Sam Levenson.

3 Everyday Health, www.everydayhealth.com/kids-

health-pictures/health-boosts-grandparents-give-their-grandchildren.aspx#/slide-1.

4 http://www.independent.co.uk/news/education/education-news/our-children-tested-to-destruc-tion-779790.html, reporting on the findings of Kathy Hall and Kamil Özerk, 'Primary Curriculum and Assessment: England and Other Countries' (2009), in Robin Alexander, *Cambridge Primary Review Research Surveys* (Routledge, 2010), pp. 375–414.

5 http://www.standard.co.uk/news/teenage-girls-would-consider-plastic-surgery-7248388.html.

6 Dr Pat Spungin of Raising Kids, quoted in 'The things that wipe the smile off young boys' faces', *The Times*, 24 May 2005, available at http://www.thetimes.co.uk/tto/news/uk/article1933337.ece.

7 http://www.dailymail.co.uk/sciencetech/article-2147871/Children-addicted-television-face-lifetime-hooked-box-say-doctors-warn-generation-risks-brain-damage.html.

8 J. Griggs, J.-P. Tan, A. Buchanan, S. Attar-Schwartz and E. Flouri, '"They've Always Been There for Me": Grandparental Involvement and Child Well-Being', *Children and Society*, vol. 24, 2010, pp. 200–14.

9 http://www.scrapbook.com/quotes/doc/21359/215.html, quoting Marcy DeMaree.

Chapter 6

1 *Forgotten Families* (Adfam/Grandparents Plus, 2006).
2 J. Hunt, S. Waterhouse and E. Lutman, *Keeping Them in the Family: Outcomes for Abused and Neglected Children Placed with Family or Friends Carers through Care Proceedings*, DCSF-RBX-05-08 (Department of Education, 2008).
3 Daycare Trust Parents' Survey 2011, available at www.daycaretrust.org.uk/data/files/final_daycare_ grandparents_2011_051.pdf.
4 Age Concern, 2004, The Economy of Older People.
5 http://www.daycaretrust.org.uk/pages/childcare-costs-survey-2012.html.
6 J. Rutter and B. Evans, *Listening to Grandparents* (Daycare Trust, 2011).

Chapter 7

1 C.S. Lewis, *The Four Loves* (Collins, 2012).
2 J. Griggs, J.-P. Tan, A. Buchanan, S. Attar-Schwartz and E. Flouri, '"They've Always Been There for Me": Grandparental Involvement and Child Well-Being', *Children and Society*, vol. 24, 2010, pp. 200–14.

Useful Organisations

Care for the Family – a national charity which aims to promote strong family life and to help those who face family difficulties.
Tel: 029 2081 0800
Website: www.careforthefamily.org.uk

Carers UK – information and support for carers of children or adults.
Tel: 0808 808 7777
Website: www.carersuk.org

Citizens Advice Bureaux – telephone, face to face and email information and advice.
Tel: To find your nearest local bureau search online via their website or in local telephone directory.
Website: www.citizensadvice.org.uk

Contact a Family – support and advice for family members who care for children with disability or special needs.

Helpline: 0808 808 3555
Website: www.cafamily.org.uk

National Family Mediation Helpline – provides information on family mediation, advice on whether your case may be suitable for mediation, information about eligibility for public funding, and contact details for mediation services in your local area.
Tel: 0300 400 636
Website: www.familymediationhelpline.co.uk

Grandparents' Association – a membership organisation providing support and advice for grandparents.
Helpline: 0845 434 9585
Specialist welfare benefits helpline: 0844 357 1033
Website: www.grandparents-association.org.uk

Grandparents Plus – a national charity which champions the role of grandparents in children's lives, especially those who take on the caring role in difficult family circumstances.
Tel: 0300 123 7015
Website: www.grandparentsplus.org.uk

Grannynet – an information, support and social networking website for grandmothers.
Website: www.grannynet.co.uk

Gransnet – an information, support and social networking website for grandparents.

Website: www.gransnet.com

Family Lives – a national charity working for and with parents that offers practical solutions and suggestions to manage their particular situations and difficulties. Dedicated to helping anyone caring for children.
Free confidential helpline: 0808 800 2222
Website: www.familylives.org.uk

PACT (Prison Advice and Care Trust) – a charity that provides practical and emotional support to prisoners' children and families and to prisoners themselves.
Helpline: 0808 808 2003
Website: www.prisonadvice.org.uk

Introducing Care for the Family

I hope that you've enjoyed reading this book, and that you feel you have gained some practical insights that will strengthen and encourage you as a grandparent.

I have mentioned Care for the Family in the book and thought you may like to hear a bit more about what we do. We are a national charity that has been working to strengthen and support family life for twenty-five years. This includes providing help and encouragement in the areas of marriage, parenting and bereavement and hundreds of thousands of families are helped each year.

Our courses are for parents of pre-school children, older children and children with additional needs; there's also a course especially for dads. We have networks of accredited befrienders who support those who are widowed early in life, bereaved parents and parents of children with additional needs.

Thousands of people have attended our events and courses and we have been privileged to be able to offer encouragement to families during the good times and be a support when times are tough. Over the years, people have told me over and over again that our books, DVDs, an event or other resources have made a real difference to them and their family.

If you are ever facing a difficult family situation, or are looking for ways to make your family relationships even stronger, then give us a call on 029 2081 0800. Much more information – including articles and advice – is available online at www.careforthefamily.org.uk

With very best wishes,

Rob Parsons

Rob Parsons, OBE
Founder and Chief Executive
Care for the Family

P.S. If you would like to help us support families and could donate to Care for the Family, or remember us in your will, please go to the donations page on our website or call us on 029 2081 0800.